普通高等教育经管类专业"十三五"规划教材

财务管理英语

王文杰 闵 雪 主 编
贺 琼 王昱睿 杜 丹 副主编

清华大学出版社
北 京

内 容 简 介

本书按财务管理专业主干课程的架构共设四篇十章,具体包括财务管理概述、财务报表概述、货币时间价值、风险与收益、资本预算、资本成本、资本结构、股利政策、资产评估概述及权益估值和公司估值等内容。本书不仅列出了各章节主要概念,配有中文的拓展阅读,用于丰富和启发学生对于相关知识点的学习,而且配有适当的习题与案例,供教师教学和学生学习使用。

本书内容全面,包含了财务管理、公司理财、资产评估及企业价值评估等专业方向的基本理论介绍,特别适合用作财务管理相关专业学生的教材,也可供相关从业者学习参考。教学课件和习题答案的下载方式见前言。

本书封面贴有清华大学出版社防伪标签,无标签者不得销售。
版权所有,侵权必究。举报: 010-62782989, beiqinquan@tup.tsinghua.edu.cn。

图书在版编目(CIP)数据

财务管理英语/王文杰,闵雪主编. —北京:清华大学出版社,2020.10(2022.1重印)
普通高等教育经管类专业"十三五"规划教材
ISBN 978-7-302-52921-7

Ⅰ.①财… Ⅱ.①王… ②闵… Ⅲ.①财务管理—英语—高等学校—教材 Ⅳ.①F275

中国版本图书馆 CIP 数据核字(2019)第 083545 号

责任编辑:崔 伟
封面设计:周晓亮
版式设计:方加青
责任校对:成凤进
责任印制:丛怀宇

出版发行:清华大学出版社
网 址:http://www.tup.com.cn,http://www.wqbook.com
地 址:北京清华大学学研大厦 A 座　　邮 编:100084
社 总 机:010-62770175　　邮 购:010-62786544
投稿与读者服务:010-62776969,c-service@tup.tsinghua.edu.cn
质 量 反 馈:010-62772015,zhiliang@tup.tsinghua.edu.cn

印 装 者:北京鑫海金澳胶印有限公司
经 销:全国新华书店
开 本:185mm×260mm　　印 张:11.5　　字 数:273 千字
版 次:2020 年 11 月第 1 版　　印 次:2022 年 1 月第 2 次印刷
定 价:42.00 元

产品编号:082327-01

前　言

随着企业的全球化经营与发展，金融市场和资本市场的竞争态势都发生着前所未有的巨大变化。企业想要求得生存并获得发展，就必须重视企业管理，而财务管理是企业管理工作中的重要一环，始终贯穿于企业管理的全过程。因此，提高企业的财务管理水平对促进企业发展、实现企业价值最大化具有重要意义。

在当今商业全球化和金融国际化的环境下，外资企业大量涌入，本土企业的国际业务激增，还有一些企业竞相赴海外上市，这些都对我国的财务管理人员提出了更高的专业要求。许多财务管理人员虽然专业知识过硬，但专业英语水平不高，具体表现为阅读英文专业资料存在障碍，惧怕编写英文财务报告，以专业英语汇报工作更是颇感为难。

目前出版的财务管理英语教材，大多是优秀的英文原版教材或翻译版教材，版本较低、内容较旧，而为数不多的非英文原版教材相对简单，未能满足财务管理专业学生的学习需求。因此，编写本书旨在帮助财务管理相关专业的学生可以系统、轻松地学习专业英语。作为一本财务管理英语的基础教材，本书具备简洁、系统、全面的特点，同时适合从事财务管理相关工作的人员作为参考书使用。

本书按财务管理专业主干课程的架构共设四篇十章，主要内容包括财务管理概述、财务报表概述、货币时间价值、风险与收益、资本预算、资本成本、资本结构、股利政策、资产评估概述、权益估值和公司估值等。各章由基本知识、核心词汇、重要概念、拓展阅读和习题组成，丰富了教学内容，并能有效地开拓学生视野。本书提供配套课件和习题答案，教师可从http://www.tupwk.com.cn下载。

本书由王文杰副教授(博士)、闵雪(博士生)担任主编，贺琼、王昱睿、杜丹担任副主编。具体编写分工如下：王文杰负责全书写作大纲的拟定和编写的组织工作，王文杰、闵雪负责编写第一章、第二章、第三章、第七章；贺琼、王昱睿、张淼、李佳钰、李佳梁、杜丹、徐佩文负责编写第四章、第五章、第六章、第八章、第九章和第十章。为了进一步提升本书的质量，东北财经大学会计学院傅荣教授作为教材主审，将其多年的教学经验与编者分享，并指导编者融入教材的内容体系中，令教材更具实用性。

在本书的编写过程中，得到了学校领导和相关部门、老师的大力支持与帮助，对此表示衷心的感谢！由于时间仓促，水平有限，本书难免存在疏漏与不足，恳请专家和读者进行批评指正。

编 者

2020年9月

目录

Part I Basis of Financial Valuation ... 1

Chapter 1 Introduction to Financial Management ... 2

1.1 Financial Management and Financial Manager ... 3
  1.1.1 Financial Management ... 3
  1.1.2 Financial Manager ... 4
1.2 Objectives and Functions of Financial Management ... 4
  1.2.1 Objectives of Financial Management ... 4
  1.2.2 Functions of Financial Management ... 6
1.3 Financial Market and Market Efficiency ... 7
  1.3.1 Financial Market ... 7
  1.3.2 Market Efficiency ... 8
  1.3.3 Degrees of Market Efficiency ... 8
1.4 Agency Relationships ... 10
  1.4.1 Agency Problems ... 10
  1.4.2 Agency Costs ... 10
  1.4.3 Practical Solutions to the Agency Problems ... 11
Questions and Problems ... 16

Chapter 2 Introduction to Financial Statements ... 18

2.1 Financial Statements and Annual Reports ... 19
  2.1.1 Overview of Financial Statements ... 19
  2.1.2 Corporate Annual Reports ... 20
2.2 Analysis of Financial Statements ... 21
  2.2.1 The Need for Ratios ... 21
  2.2.2 Types of Accounting Ratios ... 22
  2.2.3 Users of Ratios ... 22

2.2.4　Categories of Ratio ·· 23

Questions and Problems ··· 32

Chapter 3　Time Value of Money ··· 34

3.1　Value Creation and Corporate Investment ································ 35

3.2　Simple and Compound Interest ··· 36

    3.2.1　Simple Interest ··· 36

    3.2.2　Compound Interest ··· 36

3.3　Future Value and Present Value ·· 37

    3.3.1　Future Value ·· 37

    3.3.2　Present Value ·· 38

    3.3.3　Determining the Rate of Interest ··································· 39

    3.3.4　Annuity ·· 39

Questions and Problems ··· 46

Part II　Capital Budgeting ·· 47

Chapter 4　Risk and Return ··· 48

4.1　Understanding Return ·· 49

    4.1.1　Return ·· 49

    4.1.2　Measuring Return ··· 50

4.2　Understanding Risk ·· 50

    4.2.1　Risk ··· 50

    4.2.2　Measuring Risk ·· 51

4.3　Portfolio Theory ·· 52

    4.3.1　Basic Assumptions ··· 52

    4.3.2　Portfolio Return and Risk ·· 52

    4.3.3　Minimum-Variance and Efficient Frontiers ······················ 56

    4.3.4　The Selection of an Optimal Portfolio ···························· 57

    4.3.5　Systematic Risk and Unsystematic Risk ·························· 60

4.4　Capital Asset Pricing Model (CAPM) ····································· 61

Questions and Problems ··· 66

Chapter 5　Categories of Capital Budgeting Projects ···················· 69

5.1　Capital Budgeting ·· 70

5.2 Project Appraisal ··· 71
5.2.1 Categories of Capital Budgeting Projects ··· 71
5.2.2 Are Profit Calculations Useful for Estimating Project Viability? ··· 71
5.2.3 Guidelines for Estimating Project Cash Flows ··· 72

5.3 Project Appraisal Rules ··· 73
5.3.1 Net Present Value (NPV) ··· 73
5.3.2 Internal Rate of Return (IRR) ··· 74
5.3.3 Payback Period and Discounted Payback Period ··· 77
5.3.4 Accounting Rate of Return ··· 79

5.4 The Investment Process ··· 81
Questions and Problems ··· 86

Chapter 6 Cost of Capital ··· 88

6.1 Introduction to the Cost of Capital ··· 89
6.1.1 Source of Finance ··· 89
6.1.2 What is the Cost of Capital? ··· 90
6.1.3 General Model to Estimate the Cost of Capital ··· 90

6.2 Cost of Debt ··· 90

6.3 Cost of Equity ··· 91
6.3.1 Cost of Preferred Stock ··· 91
6.3.2 Cost of Common Equity ··· 92

6.4 Weighted Average Cost of Capital ··· 95
6.4.1 What is the Weighted Average Cost of Capital? ··· 95
6.4.2 Factors Affecting the Weighted Average Cost of Capital ··· 95

Questions and Problems ··· 98

Part III Financing Decision ··· 103

Chapter 7 Capital Structure ··· 104

7.1 Leverage Analysis ··· 105
7.1.1 Operating Leverage ··· 105
7.1.2 Financial Leverage ··· 106
7.1.3 Total Leverage ··· 107
7.1.4 Financial Risk and Financial Leverage ··· 108

7.2　Capital Structure and Cost of Capital ················108

7.3　Capital Structure Theory ················109

7.4　Factors that Influence a Firm's Capital Structure Decision ················110

7.5　Features of an Optimal Capital Structure ················110

7.6　Value of a Firm and Cost of Capital ················111

Questions and Problems ················115

Chapter 8　Dividend Policy ················117

8.1　Dividend Payments ················118

 8.1.1　Dividend ················118

 8.1.2　Cash Dividend, Stock Dividend and Stock Split ················118

 8.1.3　Dividends Payment ················120

8.2　Overview of Dividend Policy ················120

 8.2.1　Factors Affecting Dividend Policy ················120

 8.2.2　Residual Policy ················121

 8.2.3　Constant Dividend Payout Ratio ················121

 8.2.4　Stable Dividend Policy ················122

8.3　Share Repurchase ················122

Questions and Problems ················125

Part IV　Valuation ················129

Chapter 9　Introduction to Asset Valuation ················130

9.1　Asset Valuation ················131

 9.1.1　Definition of Asset Valuation ················131

 9.1.2　Characteristics of Asset Valuation ················132

9.2　Assumptions of Asset Valuation ················132

 9.2.1　Open Market Concepts ················132

 9.2.2　Continue to Use Concepts ················133

 9.2.3　Liquidation Concepts ················133

9.3　Types of Value ················133

 9.3.1　Market Value ················133

 9.3.2　Replacement Cost ················133

 9.3.3　Present Value ················133

  9.3.4 Liquidation Value ······ 133
9.4 Procedures of Asset Valuation ······ 134
9.5 Approaches of Asset Valuation ······ 134
  9.5.1 Market Approach ······ 134
  9.5.2 Income Approach ······ 135
  9.5.3 Cost Approach ······ 137
Questions and Problems ······ 144

Chapter 10 Equity & Corporate Valuation ······ 147

10.1 Equity Valuation ······ 148
  10.1.1 Dividends Discount Model ······ 148
  10.1.2 Free Cash Flow to Equity Discount Model ······ 152
10.2 Corporate Valuation ······ 153
  10.2.1 Free Cash Flow to the Firm Discount Model ······ 153
  10.2.2 Price-Earnings Ratio ······ 157
Questions and Problems ······ 160

Appendix I Future Value of $1 at Compound Interest ······ 164

Appendix II Present Value of $1 at Compound Interest ······ 166

Appendix III Present Value of an Annuity of $1 at Compound Interest ······ 168

Appendix IV Future Value of an Annuity of $1 at Compound Interest ······ 170

Part I
Basis of Financial Valuation

Chapter 1

Introduction to Financial Management

Introduction

To establish any business, a person must find answers to the following questions.

(1) What capital investments are required to be made? Capital investments are made to acquire the real assets, required for establishing and running the business smoothly. Real assets are land and buildings, plants and equipment etc.

(2) What decisions are to be taken on the sources from which the funds required for the capital investments mentioned above could be obtained?

(3) There are two sources of funds—debt and equity. In what proportion the funds are to be obtained from these sources is to be decided for formulating the financing plan?

(4) What decisions are to be made on the routine aspects of the day to day management of collecting money due from the firms' customers and making payments to the suppliers of various resources to the firm?

These are the core elements of the financial management of a firm. Before getting carried away with specific financial issues and technical details, it is important to gain a broad perspective by looking at the fundamental questions and the place of finance in the overall scheme of things. Conveying this broad perspective is the main aim of this chapter.

1.1 Financial Management and Financial Manager

1.1.1 Financial Management

In general, financial management is an integrated decision-making process concerned with acquiring, financing, and managing assets to accomplish some overall goal within a business entity. Financial management requires the coordination of all areas of a business to effectively benefit the owners. Within a company, financial decision-making is usually managed by the controller, treasurer, or vice-president of finance. The organization may be a business enterprise, such as a manufacturing company, an accounting firm, an oil producer, or a credit union, or it may be a charitable organization. The day-to-day purpose of financial management is to meet current and future operating needs. Other names for financial management include managerial finance, corporate finance, and business finance.

1.1.2 Financial Manager

Financial manager, also called the chief financial officer (CFO), has the primary responsibility of acquiring funds (cash) needed by a firm and for directing these funds into projects that will maximize the value of the firm for its owners. The CFO typically reports to the chief executive officer (CEO) and to the board of directors, and may additionally sit on the board. Every key decision made by a firm's managers has important financial implications. Managers face daily questions like the following:

- *Will a particular investment be profitable?*
- *Where will the funds come from to finance the investment?*
- *Does the firm have adequate cash or access to cash through bank borrowing agreements, for example, to meet its daily operating needs?*
- *Which customers should be offered credit, and how much should they be offered?*
- *How many inventories should be held?*
- *Is a merger or acquisition advisable?*
- *How should profits be used or distributed? That is, what is the optimal dividend policy?*
- *In trying to arrive at the best financial management decisions, how should risk and return be balanced?*

The decisions of all these questions need to be made with the help of a financial manager.

1.2 Objectives and Functions of Financial Management

1.2.1 Objectives of Financial Management

Effective financial decision making requires an understanding of the goals of the firm. What objectives should guide business decision making? That is, what should a manager try to achieve for the owners of the firm? The most widely accepted objective of the firm is to maximize the value of the firm for its owners; that is, to maximize shareholder wealth. Shareholder wealth is represented by the market price of a firm's common stock.

The shareholder wealth maximization goal states that management should seek to maximize the present value of the expected future returns to the owners (that is, shareholders) of the firm. These returns can take the form of periodic dividend payments or proceeds from the sale of the common stock. Present value is defined as the value today of some future payment or stream of payments, evaluated at an appropriate discount rate. The discount rate takes into account the returns that are available from alternative investment opportunities during a specific (future) time period. The longer it takes to receive a benefit, such as a cash dividend or price appreciation, the lower the value an investor places on that benefit. In addition, the greater the risk associated with receiving a future benefit, the lower the value an investor places on that benefit. Stock prices, the measure of shareholder wealth, reflect the magnitude, timing, and risk associated with future benefits expected to be received by stockholders.

Shareholder wealth is measured by the market value of the shareholders' common stock holdings. Market value is defined as the price at which the stock trades in the marketplace, such as the Shanghai Stock Exchange (SSE). Thus, total shareholder wealth equals the number of shares outstanding times the market price per share.

The objective of shareholder wealth maximization has a number of distinct advantages.

(1) This objective considers the timing and the risk of the benefits expected to be received from stock ownership. Similarly, managers must consider the elements of timing and risk as they make important financial decisions. In this way, managers can make decisions that will contribute to increasing shareholder wealth.

(2) It is conceptually possible to determine whether a particular financial decision is consistent with this objective. If a decision made by a firm has the effect of increasing the market price of the firm's stock, it is a good decision. If it appears that an action will not achieve this result, the action should not be taken.

(3) Shareholder wealth maximization is an impersonal objective. Stockholders who object to a firm's policies are free to sell theirs under more favorable terms (that is, at a higher price) and invest their funds elsewhere. If an investor who has a consumption pattern or risk preference that is not accommodated by the investment, financing, and dividend decisions of that firm, the investor will be able to sell his or her shares in that firm at the best price and purchase shares in a company that more closely meets the investor's needs.

For these reasons, the shareholder wealth maximization objective is the primary goal in financial management. Concerns for the social responsibilities of business, the existence of other objectives pursued by some managers, and problems that arise from agency relationships may cause some departures from pure wealth maximizing behavior by owners and managers. Nevertheless, the shareholder wealth maximization goal provides the standard against which actual decisions can be judged and as such, is the objective assumed in financial management analysis.

1.2.2 Functions of Financial Management

1. Estimation of Capital Requirements

A finance manager has to make an estimation with regards to the capital requirements of the company. This will depend upon expected costs and profits and future programs and policies of a concern. Estimations have to be made in an adequate manner which increases the earning capacity of an enterprise.

2. Determination of Capital Composition

Once the estimations have been made, the capital structure has to be decided. This involves short-term and long-term debt equity analysis. This will depend upon the proportion of equity capital that a company possesses and additional funds which have to be raised from outside parties.

3. Choice of Sources of Funds

For additional funds to be procured, a company has many choices like:

(1) Issue of shares and debentures;

(2) Loans to be taken from banks and financial institutions;

(3) Public deposits to be drawn like in the form of bonds.

The choice will depend on the relative merits and demerits of each source and period of financing.

4. Investment of Funds

The finance manager has to decide to allocate funds into profitable ventures so that there is safety on investment and regular returns are possible.

5. Disposal of Surplus

The net profits decision has to be made by the finance manager. This can be done in two ways:

(1) Dividend declaration — it includes identifying the rate of dividends and other benefits like bonus.

(2) Retained profits — the volume has to be decided which will depend upon expansion, innovational and diversification plans of the company.

6. Management of Cash

The finance manager has to make decisions with regard to cash management. Cash is required for many purposes like payment of wages and salaries, payment of electricity and water bills, payment to creditors, meeting current liabilities, maintenance of enough stock,

Introduction to Financial Management — Chapter 1

purchase of raw materials, etc.

7. Financial Controls

The finance manager has not only to plan, procure and utilize the funds, but also to exercise control over finances. This can be done through many techniques like ratio analysis, financial forecasting, cost and profit control, etc.

1.3 Financial Market and Market Efficiency

1.3.1 Financial Market

A financial market is a broad term describing any marketplace where buyers and sellers participate in the trade of assets such as equities, bonds, currencies and derivatives. Financial markets are typically defined by having transparent pricing, basic regulations on trading, costs and fees, and market forces determining the prices of securities that trade.

Financial markets can be found in nearly every nation in the world. Some are very small, with only a few participants, while others — like the New York Stock Exchange (NYSE) and the foreign exchange markets — trade trillions of dollars daily.

Investors have access to a large number of financial markets and exchanges representing a vast array of financial products. Some of these markets have always been open to private investors; others remained the exclusive domain of major international banks and financial professionals until the very end of the twentieth century. Common financial markets are as follows:

1. Money Markets

The money markets are wholesale markets which enable borrowing on a short-term basis. The banks are particular active in this market — both as lenders and as borrowers.

2. Bond Markets

A bond is merely a document that sets out the borrower's promise to pay sums of money in the future — usually regular interest plus a capital amount upon the maturity of the bond. There are long-dated securities issued by a variety of organizations including governments and corporations.

3. Foreign Exchange Markets

These are the markets in which one currency is exchanged for another.

4. Share Markets

A stock market, equity market or share market is the aggregation of buyers and sellers of shares (also called stock), which represents ownership claims on businesses; this may include securities listed on a public stock exchange as well as those only traded privately.

5. Derivative Markets

The derivative market is the financial market for derivatives, financial instruments like futures contracts or options, which are derived from other forms of assets.

1.3.2 Market Efficiency

A central theme of much of the academic finance and financial economics research since the 1960s has been the efficiency of the capital markets. The more efficient capital markets are, the more likely it is that resources will find their highest (risk-adjusted) return uses. Capital market efficiency is an implicit assumption in many decision models used widely in finance. Consequently, this concept is important to a full understanding of these decision models.

In an efficient capital market, stock prices provide an unbiased estimate of the true value of an enterprise. Stock prices reflect a present value estimate of the firm's expected cash flow, evaluated at an appropriate required rate of return. The required rate of return is determined by conditions in the financial markets, including the supply of funds from savers, the investment demands for funds, and expectations regarding future inflation rates. The required rate of return to a security also depends on the seniority of the security, the maturity of that security, the business and financial risk of the firm issuing the security, the risk of default, and the marketability of the security.

The efficiency of the capital markets is the important "glue" that bonds the present value of a firm's net cash flow, discounted at the appropriate risk-adjusted required rate of return, to shareholder wealth, as measured by the market value of a company's common stock. Hence, in this final section of the chapter, the concept of market efficiency is defined, the evidence regarding the extent of capital market efficiency briefly is reviewed, and some important implications of market efficiency are identified.

1.3.3 Degrees of Market Efficiency

Three levels of market efficiency have been identified, based on the information set under consideration: weak-form efficiency, semi-strong form efficiency, and strong-form efficiency.

1. Weak-form Efficiency

With weak-form market efficiency, no investor expects to earn excess returns based on an investment strategy using such information as historical price or return information. All stock market information, including the record of past stock price changes and stock trading volume, is fully reflected in the current price of a stock.

Tests of the weak-form market efficiency hypothesis have included statistical tests of independence of stock price changes from various day-to-day periods. These studies have concluded that stock price changes over time essentially are independent and that the knowledge of past price changes cannot be used to predict future changes. Other tests have looked for the existence of longer-term cycles in stock price, such as monthly or seasonal cycles. In addition, there have been tests of numerous trading rules based solely on past market price and volume information. Pinches, in a review of much of this research, has concluded that "with some exceptions, the studies of mechanical trading rules do not indicate that profits can be generated by these rules". In conclusion, the weight of the evidence indicates that U. S. capital markets are efficient in a weak-form contest.

2. Semi-strong Form Efficiency

With semi-strong form market efficiency, no investor can expect to earn excess returns based on an investment strategy using any publicly available information. Announcements of earnings changes, stock splits, dividend changes, interest rate changes, money supply levels, changes in accounting practices that affect a firm's cash flow, takeover announcements, and so on are quickly and unbiasedly incorporated in the price of a security. A finding of semi-strong form market efficiency implies that the market is also weakly efficient, because the information set considered in the weak-form case is also publicly available.

Once information is made public in a semi-strong form efficient capital market, it is impossible for investors to earn excess returns (after considering trading costs) from transactions based upon this information, because the security price will already reflect accurately the value of this information. Studies of stock split, new issues, stock listing announcements, earnings and dividends announcements, stock acquisition announcements, and announcements of analyst recommendations support the notion of semi-strong form market efficiency, at least after the cost of commissions on transactions are considered.

3. Strong-form Efficiency

With strong-form market efficiency, security prices fully reflect all information, both public and private. Thus, in a strong-form efficient capital market, no individual or group of individuals should be able consistently to earn above-normal profits, including insiders possessing information about the economic prospects of a firm.

1.4 Agency Relationships

An agency relationship is created when decision-making authority is delegated to an agent without the agent being fully responsible for the decision that is made. An agency relationship occurs in two common corporate scenarios:

(1) the company's stockholders delegate decision-making authority to the manager (agents), but the managers do not receive the full benefit or bear the full cost of their decisions.

(2) the company's debt holders delegate authority to managers who act on behalf of the shareholders.

Thus in many firms we have what is called a separation, or a divorce, of ownership and control. In times past the directors would usually be the same individuals as the owners. Today, however, less than 1 percent of the shares of most of the UK's 100 largest firms are owned by the directors.

1.4.1 Agency Problems

The separation of the ownership and control raises worries that the management team may pursue objectives attractive to them, but which are not necessarily beneficial to the shareholders. Agency problems exist between stockholders and managers because management will not beat the full impact of their decisions since they do not own 100 percent of the company. Managers may think a corporate jet or fancy offices are great ideas, as long as they are purchased with shareholder's money. Agency problems may also exist between creditors and corporations. Creditors lend money based on specific business and financial risk expectations. The stockholders may invest that money into high-risk projects for their own interest. This conflict is an example of agency problems. Given widely dispersed share ownership in today's modern company, it is virtually impossible for shareholders to monitor the day-to-day actions of managers.

1.4.2 Agency Costs

These agency problems give rise to a number of agency costs, which are incurred by shareholders to minimize agency problems. agency costs include:

(1) Expenditures to structure the organization in such a way as to minimize the incentives for managers to take actions contrary to shareholder interests, such as providing a portion of a manager's compensation in the form of stock in the corporation.

(2) Expenditures to monitor management's actions, such as paying for audits of

managerial performance and internal audits of the firm's expenditures.

(3) Bonding expenditures to protect the owners from managerial dishonesty.

(4) The opportunity cost of lost profits arising from complex organizational structures that prevents management from making timely responses to opportunities.

1.4.3 Practical Solutions to the Agency Problems

There are four methods to motivate managers to act in the best interests of shareholders.

1. Managerial Compensation

The total managerial salary package must compensate managers for their performance. This is commonly done through annual performance bonuses and long-term stock options, in addition to an annual salary. There are two main methods that are used to grant shares to management:

(1) Performance shares. Here, the manager receives a certain number of shares based on the company achieving predefined performance benchmarks (e.g. earnings or sales).

(2) Executive stock options. In this case, management is granted an option to buy the firm's shares at a pre-specified price (the exercise price) on a specific future date (the options' expiration). Executive stock options are typically issued out-of-the-money (meaning that the exercise price is high relative to the current stock price) to give management the incentive to take actions that will boost the company's stock price.

With options and performance shares, the interests of management and shareholders are aligned because both groups are focusing on the same criteria — stock price.

2. Direct Shareholder Intervention

As large institutions increasingly own shares, these institutions have the power and sophistication to persuasively intervene on corporate issues.

3. Threat of Being Fired

Shareholders can nominate and elect their own board of directors or persuade the board to encourage the current management to quit or be fired.

4. Threat of Acquisition

If management's poor performance is reflected in a low stock price, a competitor may buy enough shares to have a controlling interest. At that point, the acquirer can replace management with their own management team.

Core Words

business	企业，商业，业务
asset	资产
financial management	财务管理
decision making	决策
chief financial officer (CFO)	首席财务官
chief executive officer (CEO)	首席执行官
board of directors	董事会
stockholder/shareholder	股东
shareholder wealth	股东财富
capital structure	资本结构
allocate	(资源、权力等) 配置
creditor	债权人
liability	负债
international bank	国际银行
money market	货币市场
bond market	债券市场
foreign exchange market	外汇市场
share market	股票市场
derivative market	金融衍生品市场
financial risk	财务风险
agency problem	代理问题
separation of ownership and control	所有权与经营权分离
agency relationship	代理关系
agency cost	代理成本

Key Concepts

1. Financial managers contribute to a firm's success primarily through investment and financial decisions. Their knowledge of financial markets, investment appraisal methods,

cash management, value management and risk management techniques are vital for company growth and stability.

2. Firms should clearly define objectives of the enterprise to provide a focus for decision making.

3. The markets:
- The money markets are short-term wholesale lending and/or borrowing markets.
- The bond markets deal in long-term bond debt issued by corporations, governments, etc.
- The foreign exchange market — one currency is exchanged for another.
- The share market — primary and secondary trading in companies' shares takes place.
- The derivatives market is the financial market for derivatives, financial instruments like futures contracts or options.

4. In financial markets, the impacts of different information on prices is different. The efficiency of financial markets is divided into three types: weak-form efficiency, semi-strong form efficiency and strong-form efficiency.

5. The assumed objective of the firm for finance is to maximize shareholder wealth. Reasons include: this objective considers the timing and the risk of the benefits expected to be received from stock ownership; it is conceptually possible to determine whether a particular financial decision is consistent with this objective and it is an impersonal objective.

6. Large corporations usually have a separation of ownership and control. This may lead to managerialism where the agents take decisions primarily with their interests in mind rather than those of the shareholders. This is an agent problem. Solutions include: link managerial rewards to shareholder wealth improvement, sackings, selling shares and the threat of takeover, corporate governance regulation, improve information flow.

Extended Reading

财务管理的基本理论

在财务管理学科的发展过程中，形成了一系列基本理论，对财务管理实务起着指导作用。下面简要介绍四种基本理论，分别是现金流量理论、价值评估理论、投资组合理论和资本结构理论。

一、现金流量理论

现金流量理论是关于现金、现金流量和自由现金流量的理论，是财务管理中最基础的理论。

现金是公司流动性最强的资产，是公司生存的"血液"，"现金为王"已被广泛认知。持有现金的多寡体现了公司的流动性、支付能力、偿债能力的强弱，进而在一定程度上影响到公司的风险和价值。现金也是计量现金流量和自由现金流量的基础要素。在实务中，公司必然重视现金和现金管理。

现金流量包括现金流入量、现金流出量和现金净流量。对于公司整体及其经营活动、投资活动和筹资活动等都需要计量现金流量，进行现金流量分析、现金预算和现金控制。依据现金流量，建成现金流量折现模型，取代了过去使用的收益折现模型，可用于证券投资、项目投资的价值评估。随着研究的深化，现金流量又进化为自由现金流量。

自由现金流量(free cash flows)是指真正剩余的、可自由支配的现金流量。自由现金流量是由美国西北大学拉巴波特、哈佛大学詹森等学者于1986年提出的，历经30多年的发展，特别是在以美国安然、世通等为代表的之前在财务报表中利润指标完美无瑕的所谓"绩优公司"纷纷破产后，以自由现金流量为基础的现金流量折现模型，已成为价值评估领域最健全、使用最广泛的评估模式。

需要指出的是，财务学意义上的"现金流量"与会计学现金流量表中的"现金流量"不尽相同，主要体现在以下几个方面：

(1) 在计量口径方面，会计学现金流量包含现金等价物，而财务学现金流量则不含现金等价物。

(2) 在计量对象方面，会计学现金流量是就企业整体进行计量，而财务学现金流量不仅就企业整体进行计量，还就证券投资、项目投资等分别进行计量，为企业价值评估、证券价值评估和项目投资评价提供依据。

(3) 在计量分类方面，会计学现金流量分别对经营活动、投资活动和筹资活动进行计量；而财务学现金流量的计量分类，对证券投资分别计量其现金流入、现金流出和现金净流量，对项目投资则分别计量其初始现金流量、营业现金流量和终结现金流量。

二、价值评估理论

价值评估理论是关于内在价值、净增加值和价值评估模型的理论，是财务管理的一个核心理论。

从财务学的角度，价值主要是指内在价值、净增加值。譬如，股票的价值实质上是指股票的内在价值即现值，项目的价值实质上是指项目的净增加值即净现值。内在价值、净增加值是以现金流量为基础的折现估计值，而非精确值。

现金流量折现模型和自由现金流量折现模型是对特定证券现值和特定项目净现值的评估模型。从投资决策的角度，证券投资者需要评估特定证券的现值，据以与其市场价格比较，做出相应的决策；项目投资者需要评估待定项目的净现值，据以取得和比较净增加值的多少，做出相应的决策。

为了评估价值，还需要折现率。资本资产定价模型就是用于估计折现率的模型。资本资产定价模型由美国财务学家威廉·夏普在20世纪60年代创建。按照该模型，金融资产投资的风险分为两类：一种是可以通过分散投资来化解的可分散风险(非系统风险)，另一种是不可以通过分散投资化解的不可分散风险(系统风险)。在有效市场中，可分散风险得不到市场的补偿，只有不可分散风险能够得到补偿。个别证券的不可分散风险可以用 β 系数来计量，β 系数可计量该证券与市场组合回报率的敏感程度。市场组合是指包含市场上全部证券的投资组合。据此，形成了资本资产定价模型。资本资产定价模型解决了股权资本成本的计量问题，为确定加权平均资本成本扫清了障碍，进而使得计算现值和净现值成为可能。

三、投资组合理论

投资组合是指投资于若干种证券，其收益等于这些证券的加权平均收益，但其风险并不等于这些证券的加权平均风险。投资组合能降低非系统性风险。

投资组合理论的奠基人是美国经济学家马科维茨。他在1952年首次提出投资组合理论，并进行了系统、深入和卓有成效的研究。

从资本市场的历史中，人们认识到风险和报酬存在某种关系：一是承担风险会得到回报，这种回报称为风险溢价；二是风险性越高，风险溢价越大。但是，人们长期没有找到两者的函数关系。

马科维茨把投资组合的价格变化视为随机变量，以其均值来衡量收益，以其方差来衡量风险，揭示了投资组合风险和报酬的函数关系。因此，马克维茨的理论又称为均值-方差分析。他是第一个对"投资分散化"理念进行定量分析的经济学家，他认为通过投资分散化可以在不改变投资组合预期收益的情况下降低风险，也可以在不改变投资组合风险的情况下增加收益。

四、资本结构理论

资本结构是指公司各种长期资本的构成及比例关系。公司的长期资本包括企业的长期负债、普通股和优先股。

资本结构理论是关于资本结构与财务风险、资本成本以及公司价值之间关系的理论。资本结构理论主要有MM理论、权衡理论、代理理论和优序融资理论。

Questions and Problems

Choose the best answer to the following questions.

1. The commonly accepted goal of financial management is to ( ).

   A. maximize short-term earnings.   B. maximize shareholder wealth.

   C. minimize risk.   D. maximize international sales.

2. In agency theory, when shareholders choose to elect their own board members and replace management, this is called ( ).

   A. poison pill.   B. threat of firing.

   C. threat of takeover.   D. shareholder replacement.

3. With respect to the shareholder/manager relationship, which of the following statements is FALSE? ( )

   A. Performance shares can be used to align manager/shareholder interests.

   B. Executive stock options do not have expiration dates and are held in perpetuity.

   C. Executive stock options tend to be issued out-of-the-money.

   D. The managerial salary package should include an incentive component.

4. Which of the following is not a form of corporate control that could reduce agency problems for a public company? ( )

   A. stock options.   B. hostile takeover threat.

   C. investor monitoring.   D. all of the above.

5. Which of the following statements is NOT a mechanism to reduce the agency problem and motivate managers? ( )

   A. Poison Pill.   B. Threat of firing.

   C. Threat of takeover.   D. Managerial compensation.

6. Which of the following statements is FALSE in the shareholder/debtor relationship? ( )

   A. Debtor is the principal, because they have delegated authority to management.

   B. Shareholder and debtor interests are increasingly aligned as the company takes on more debt.

   C. Interests of the firm's management tend to be aligned more closely with those of the firm's shareholders.

   D. Shareholders have an incentive to take on risky projects because they get to keep the residual earnings of the firm.

7. No investor expects to earn excess returns based on an investment strategy using such information as historical price or return information in a (　) market.

  A. weak form efficiency. B. semi-strong form efficiency.

  C. strong form efficiency. D. None of the above efficiency.

8. Which of the following types of decision makers use accounting information to make financial decisions? (　)

  A. Investors. B. Creditors.

  C. Business owners. D. All of the above.

9. Which of the following is financial market? (　)

  A. Money market. B. Foreign exchange market.

  C. Derivative market. D. All of the above.

10. Financial Management is also called (　).

  A. corporate finance. B. financial accounting.

  C. management accounting. D. business finance.

Short answer questions.

1. Briefly explain the main types of financial decisions a firm has to deal with.

2. Briefly explain the role of the following:

  a. The money markets.

  b. The bond markets.

  c. The foreign exchange markets.

  d. The share markets.

  e. The derivatives market.

3. How can "goal congruence" for managers and shareholders be achieved?

4. Explain the rationale for selecting shareholder wealth maximization as the objective of the firm. Include a consideration of profit maximization as an alternative goal.

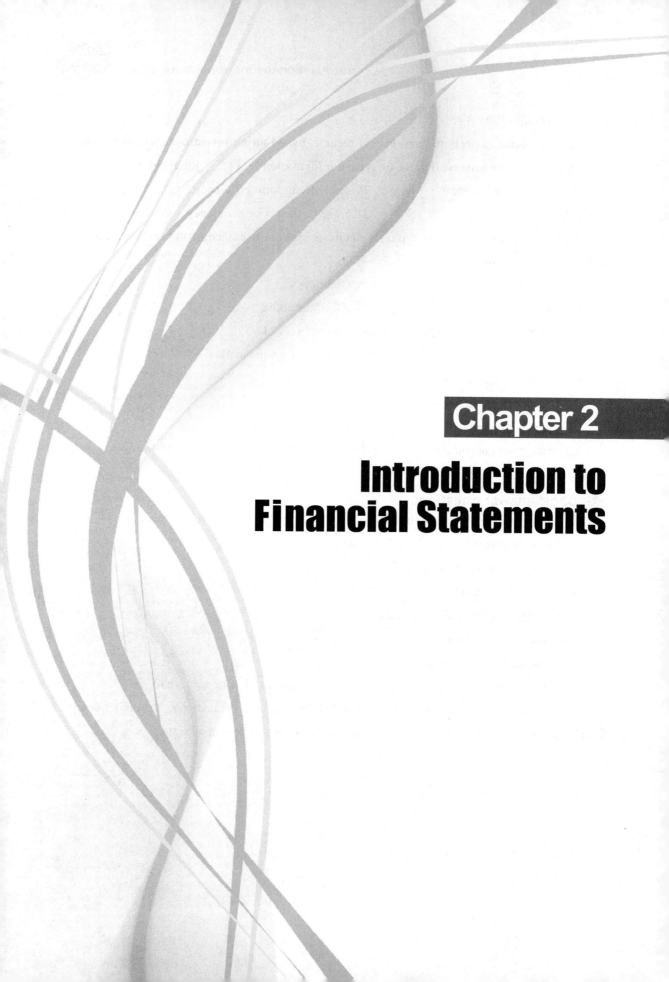

Chapter 2

Introduction to Financial Statements

Introduction to Financial Statements — Chapter 2

Introduction

Whether you watch analysts on *Financial Times* or read articles in *The Wall Street Journal*, you will hear experts insisting on the importance of "doing your homework" before investing in a company. In other words, investors should dig deep into the company's financial statements and analyze everything from the auditor's report to the footnotes. But what does this advice really mean and how do investors follow it?

The aim of this chapter is to answer these questions by providing a succinct yet advanced overview of financial statement analysis. If you already have a grasp of the definition of the balance sheet and the structure of an income statement, this chapter will give you a deeper understanding of how to analyze these reports and how to identify the "red flags" and "gold nuggets" of a company. In other words, it will teach you the important factors that make or break an investment decision.

2.1 Financial Statements and Annual Reports

2.1.1 Overview of Financial Statements

Financial statements (or financial reports) are formal records of the financial activities and position of a business, person, or other entities.

Relevant financial information is presented in a structured manner and in a form easy way to understand. It typically includes basic financial statements, accompanied by a management discussion and analysis:

(1) A statement of financial position, also referred to as a balance sheet, reports on a company's assets, liabilities, and owner's equity at a given point in time.

(2) An income statement, also known as a statement of comprehensive income, statement of revenue & expense, profit and loss report or P&L, reports on a company's income, expenses, and profits over a period of time. A profit and loss statement provides information on the operation of the enterprise. These include sales and the various expenses incurred during the stated period.

(3) A statement of changes in equity, also known as equity statement or statement of retained earnings, reports on the changes in equity of the company during the stated period.

(4) A cash flow statement reports on a company's cash flow activities, particularly its operating, investing and financing activities.

For large corporations, these statements may be complex and may include an extensive set of footnotes to the financial statements and management discussion and analysis. The notes typically describe each item on the balance sheet, income statement and cash flow statement in further detail. Notes to financial statements are considered an integral part of the financial statements.

2.1.2 Corporate Annual Reports

Annual reports are some comprehensive reports on a company's activities throughout the preceding year. Annual reports are intended to give shareholders and other interested people information about the company's activities and financial performance. They may be considered as grey literature. Most jurisdictions require companies to prepare and disclose annual reports, and many require the annual reports to be filed at the company's registry. Companies listed on a stock exchange are also required to report at more frequent intervals (depending upon the rules of the stock exchange involved).

Typical annual reports will include:
- General corporate information
- Operating and financial review
- Director's report
- Corporate governance information
- Chairman's statement
- Auditor's report
- Contents: non-audited information
- Financial statements, including:
  - Balance sheet also known as statement of financial position
  - Income statement also known as profit and loss statement.
  - Statement of changes in equity
  - Cash flow statement
- Notes to the financial statements
- Accounting policies
- Other features

Other information deemed relevant to stakeholders may be included, such as a report on operations for manufacturing firms or corporate social responsibility reports for companies with environmentally or socially sensitive operations. In the case of larger companies, it is usually a sleek, colorful, high-gloss publication.

The details provided with the report are of use to investors to understand the company's financial position and future direction. The financial statements are usually compiled in compliance with IAS, IFRS and/or the domestic GAAP, as well as domestic legislation (e.g. the SOX in the United States).

In the United States, a more-detailed version of the report, called a Form 10-K, is submitted to the United States Securities and Exchange Commission. A publicly held company may also issue a much more limited version of an annual report, which is known as a "wrap report". A wrap report is a Form 10-K with an annual report cover wrapped around it.

2.2 Analysis of Financial Statements

As we explained before, the purpose of preparing financial statements is to provide users with information which will help them to make better economic decision. Confronted with a set of financial statements, a user will need to analyze the information provided and draw some conclusions about the financial performance and position of the business concerned.

There are several ways in which financial statements might be analyzed. In practice, one of the most important methods is the technique known as ratio analysis, which involves the calculation of a number of accounting ratios. The main purpose of this part is to introduce some of the most commonly used accounting ratios and to explain the significance of each ratio.

2.2.1 The Need for Ratios

Without ratios, financial statements would be largely uninformative to all but the very skilled. With ratios, financial statements can be interpreted and usefully applied to satisfy the needs of the reader. For example, let's take the performance of four companies, all dealing in the same type of goods:

Items	Gross Profit ($)	Sales ($)
Company A	200,000	848,000
Company B	300,000	1,252,000
Company C	500,000	1,927,500
Company D	350,000	1,468,400

Suppose you want to know which company gets the "best" profit. Simply inspecting these figures and trying to decide which performance was the best, and which was the worst, is virtually impossible. To bring the same basis of comparison to each company we need some form of common measure. We can use one measure commonly used ratio — the gross margin, i.e. the amount of gross profit on sales as a percentage. Applying this to these four companies, we find that their margins are:

Company A	23.58%
Company B	23.96%
Company C	25.94%
Company D	23.84%

On this basis, Company C with a gross margin of 25.94%, in other words, $25.94 gross profit per $100 sales, has performed better than the other companies.

2.2.2 Types of Accounting Ratios

In theory, it would be possible to calculate literally hundreds of accounting ratios from a given set of financial statements. Some of these ratios would not mean very much but many of them might serve a useful purpose. In practice, however, it is usually sufficient to calculate a fairly small number of key ratios and each of these ratios is described in this part. They can be classified into three main groups:

(1) Profitability ratios. The profitability ratios measure the profit or operating success of an entity for a given period of time.

(2) Liquidity ratios. The liquidity ratios measure the short-term ability of an entity to pay its maturing obligations and to meet unexpected need for cash.

(3) Solvency ratios. Solvency ratios measure the ability of an entity to survive over a long period of time.

2.2.3 Users of Ratios

As you know, there are a great many parties interested in analyzing financial statements, including shareholders, lenders, customers, suppliers, employees, government agencies and competitors. Yet, in many respects, they will be interested in different things. Nevertheless, it is possible to construct a series of ratios that together will provide all of them with something that they will find relevant and from which they can investigate further if necessary.

Table 2-1 shows some categories of ratios and indicates some of the stakeholders' groups that would be interested in them.

Table 2-1 Users of ratios

Ratio category	Examples of interested groups
Profitability	Shareholders, management, employees, creditors, competitors, potential investors
Liquidity	Shareholders, suppliers, creditors, competitors
Solvency	Shareholders, potential investors, creditors

2.2.4 Categories of Ratio

1. Profitability Ratios

(1) Return on Ordinary Shareholders' Equity (ROE)

A widely used measure of profitability from the perspective of the ordinary shareholder is the return on ordinary shareholders' equity. This ratio shows the amount of profit earned for each dollar invested by the shareholders. The ratio is calculated as follows:

$$ROE = \frac{Profit\ available\ to\ ordinary\ shareholders}{Average\ ordinary\ shareholders\ equity}$$

To determine the profit available to ordinary shareholders, we need to subtract any dividends for preference shareholders. A higher ROE appears more attractive investment to potential investors as it provides the greater return on shareholder funds invested.

(2) Return on Assets (ROA)

The return on ordinary shareholders' equity is affected by two factors: the return on assets (ROA) and the degree of leverage. The return on assets ratio measures the overall profitability of assets in terms of the profit earned on each dollar invested in assets. The ratio is calculated as follows:

$$ROA = \frac{Profit\ after\ tax}{Average\ total\ assets}$$

It is a measure of management's effectiveness based on normal business activities. The higher the return on assets, the more profitable the entity.

(3) Profit Margin

The return on asset is affected by two factors, the first of which is the profit margin. The profit margin, or rate of return on sales, is a measure of the amount of each dollar of sales that results in profit.

$$Profit\ margin = \frac{Profit\ after\ tax}{Net\ sales}$$

Profit margin varies from industry to industry, as can be seen in the following hypothetical business examples. High-volume businesses such as supermarkets generally experience low profit margins, which can be below 7 cents (7%). In contrast, some industries such as hotels, restaurants and leisure industry, had a higher profit margin of 14 cents (14%) approximately.

(4) Asset Turnover

The other factor that affects the return on assets is the asset turnover. The asset turnover measures how efficiently an entity uses its assets to generate sales. It is determined by dividing net sales by average total assets for the period. The resulting number shows the dollar of sales produced by each dollar invested in assets.

$$Asset\ turnover = \frac{Net\ sales}{Average\ total\ assets}$$

Asset turnovers vary considerably across different industry sectors. For example, Hilton Hotels & Resorts, which operates in the hotels, restaurants and leisure industry, had a low turnover ratio. In contrast, Music and Games Ltd, which operates in the specialty retail industry, had a high asset turnover.

(5) Gross Profit Margin

Two factors strongly influence the profit margin. One is the gross profit margin. The profit margin is determined by dividing gross profit by net sales. This rate indicates an entity's ability to maintain an adequate selling price above its costs. As an industry becomes more competitive, this ratio declines. The ratio is calculated as follows:

$$Gross\ profit\ margin = \frac{Gross\ profit}{Net\ Sales}$$

It would be very misleading to compare the gross profit margin of two totally dissimilar businesses but a comparison between two companies in the same line of trade should be meaningful and might throw some light on the pricing policies adopted by each of the companies concerned.

(6) Operating Expenses to Sales Ratio

This is the other factor that directly affects the profit margin. Management can influence an entity's profitability by maintaining adequate prices, cutting expenses, or both. The operating expenses to sales ratio measures the costs incurred to support each dollar of sales.

$$Operating\ expenses\ to\ sales\ ratio = \frac{Operating\ expenses}{Net\ Sales}$$

An alternative approach is to include finance costs as well as the expenses used in the formula provided above. However, when comparing the operating expenses to sales ratios of different entities, it is preferable to exclude finance costs so that the comparison is not distorted by differences in financial structure.

(7) Earnings Per Share (EPS)

Shareholders usually think in terms of the number of shares they own or plan to buy or sell. Expressing profit earned on a per share basis provides a useful perspective for determining profitability. Earnings per share is a measure of the profit earned on each ordinary share.

$$Earnings\ per\ share = \frac{Profit\ available\ to\ ordinary\ shareholders}{Weighted\ average\ number\ of\ ordinary\ shares}$$

When we use earnings per share, it refers to the amount of profit applicable to each ordinary share. Therefore, when we calculate earnings per share, if there are preference dividends declared for the period, they must be deducted from profit to determine the profit available to the ordinary shareholders.

Higher earnings per share is always better than a lower ratio because this means the company is more profitable and the company has more profits to distribute to its shareholders. Although many investors don't pay much attention to the EPS, a higher earnings per share ratio often makes the stock price of a company rise. Since so many things can manipulate this ratio, investors tend to look at it but don't let it influence their decisions drastically.

(8) Price/Earnings Ratio (P/E Ratio)

Like EPS, the price/earnings ratio is another statistic that is often quoted as it measures the ratio of the market price of each ordinary share to the earnings per share. The price/earnings ratio is a reflection of investors' assessment of a company's future earnings and indicates how much an investor would have to pay in the market for each dollar of earnings expected.

$$Price/earnings\ ratio = \frac{Market\ price\ per\ ordinary\ share}{Earnings\ per\ share}$$

It might appear that shares with a low P/E ratio would be regarded as an attractive investment. In fact, high P/E ratios are usually viewed more favorably than low ones. This is because the market price of a share reflects the stock market's expectations of the company's future performance. Therefore, a high P/E ratio is seen as an indication that the company's shares will perform well in the future.

(9) Dividend Yield Ratio

The dividend yield ratio expresses the dividend per ordinary share as a percentage of the market price per ordinary share. The calculation is as follows:

$$Dividend\ yield\ ratio = \frac{Dividends\ per\ ordinary\ share}{Market\ price\ per\ ordinary\ share} \times 100\%$$

This ratio acts as an indicator of the cash return received on the investment made by an ordinary shareholder. Whilst a low dividend yield might deter an investor who views the shares primarily as a source of income, a dividend yields of even 0% might not deter an investor whose main concern is capital growth.

2. Liquidity Ratios

(1) Current Ratio

The purpose of the current ratio is to measure the company's ability to meet its short-term financial obligations out of its current assets. The current ratio is usually expressed as an actual ratio and is calculated as follows:

$$Current\ ratio = \frac{Current\ assets}{Current\ liabilities}$$

What is perceived as an acceptable level of current ratio will vary from one type of business to another. For example, a ratio of 1∶1 may be perfectly adequate for a supermarket chain which has virtually no debtors and which rapidly converts its stocks into cash. On the other hand, a ratio of at least 2∶1 might be seen as necessary for a manufacturing company which holds stocks for a longer period and then sells them on credit terms.

(2) Quick Ratio (or Acid Test Ratio)

In many cases, a company's stocks cannot be converted into cash at short notice and therefore the current ratio (which takes all current assets into account) may give an over-optimistic view of the company's liquidity. The quick ratio provides a more severe test of liquidity by omitting stocks from the calculation. The ratio is calculated as follows:

$$Quick\ ratio = \frac{Current\ assets - Inventory}{Current\ liabilities}$$

Although a quick ratio of at least 1∶1 might be seen as desirable, it should be borne in mind that some of the current liabilities shown in a company's balance sheet might not be payable immediately. For instance, the corporation tax liability does not fall due until five months after the end of the accounting year. In these circumstances, a ratio of less than 1∶1 might be acceptable. Note that the quick ratio is also known as the acid test ratio.

(3) Accounts Receivable Turnover Ratio

Accounts receivable turnover ratio is an accounting measure used to measure how effective a company is in extending credit as well as collecting debts. The receivables turnover ratio is an activity ratio, measuring how efficiently a firm uses its assets. The ratio is calculated as follows:

$$\text{Accounts receivable turnover ratio} = \frac{\text{Net credit sales}}{\text{Average accounts receivable}}$$

A high ratio implies either that a company operates on a cash basis or that its extension of credit and collection of accounts receivable is efficient. While a low ratio implies the company is not making the timely collection of credit.

(4) Average Collection Period

This is a variation of the receivables turnover which converts the turnover into an average collection period in days. This is done by dividing the receivable turnover into 365 days.

$$\text{Average collection period} = \frac{365 \text{ days}}{\text{Accounts receivables turnover}}$$

The ratio can be used to assess the effectiveness of an entity's credit and collection policies. A general rule is that the collection period should not greatly exceed the credit term period, which is the time allowed for payment.

(5) Inventory Turnover

Inventory turnover measures how efficient a business is at maintaining an appropriate level of inventory. When it is not being as efficient as it used to be, or is being less efficient than its competitors, this may indicate that control over inventory levels in being undermined.

A reduction in inventory turnover can mean that the business is slowing down. Inventory may be piling up and not being sold. This could lead to a liquidity crisis, as money may be taken out of the bank simply to increase inventory which is not then sold quickly enough. The ratio is calculated as follows:

$$\text{Inventory turnover ratio} = \frac{\text{Cost of goods sold}}{\text{Average inventory}}$$

A high inventory turnover ratio, relative to some benchmark, suggests efficient management of the firm's inventory. A low inventory ratio, declining ratio may suggest the firm has continued to build up inventory in face of weakening demand or may be carrying and reporting outdated or obsolete inventory that could only be sold at reduced prices, if at all.

(6) Average Days in Inventory

This is a variation of the inventory turnover that converts the turnover into days. This is done by dividing the inventory turnover by 365 days. The average days in inventory ratio measures the average number of days it takes to sell the inventory.

$$\text{Average days in inventory} = \frac{365 \text{ days}}{\text{Inventory turnover}}$$

Average days in inventory vary considerably across different industry sectors. An inventory turnover of 100 days may be acceptable for non-perishable items such as computers or furniture but a much higher turnover would be necessary for perishables such as fresh food items.

3. Solvency Ratios

(1) Debt to Total Assets Ratio

The debt to total assets ratio measures the percentage of the total assets financed by creditors. It is calculated by dividing total liabilities by total assets.

$$Debt\ to\ total\ assets\ ratio = \frac{Total\ liabilities}{Total\ assets}$$

This ratio indicates the degree of leveraging; it provides some indication of the entity's ability to withstand losses without impairing the interests of its creditors. The higher the percentage of total liabilities to total assets, the greater the financial risk that the entity may be unable to meet its maturing obligations. The lower the debt to total assets ratio, the greater the equity available to creditors if the entity becomes insolvent. Therefore, from the creditors' point of view, a low ratio of debt to total assets is usually desirable.

(2) Time Interest Earned

Time interest earned (also called interest coverage) indicates the entity's ability to meet interest payments as they come due. It is calculated by dividing earnings before income tax plus interest expense (finance costs) by interest expense.

$$Time\ interest\ earned = \frac{Earnings\ before\ interest\ and\ tax}{Interest\ expense}$$

Note that this ratio uses earnings before income tax and interest expense (EBIT) because this amount represents what is available to cover interest. A general rule of thumb is that earnings should be approximately 3~4 times the interest expense.

(3) Cash Debt Coverage

Net cash provided by operating activities to average total liabilities, called the cash debt coverage, is a cash-bases measure of solvency. This ratio indicates an entity's ability to repay its liabilities from cash generated from operating activities, without having to liquidate the assets used in its operations.

$$Cash\ debt\ coverage = \frac{Net\ cash\ provided\ by\ operating\ activities}{Average\ total\ liabilities}$$

While what is considered an acceptable ratio varies between industries, a general rule of thumb is that a ratio between 0.20 times is considered cause for additional investigation.

Core Words

financial statement	财务报表
statement of financial position (balance sheet)	资产负债表
income statement (statement of profit or loss, statement of comprehensive income)	利润表
owner's equity	所有者权益
statement of changes in equity	权益变动表
statement of cash flows (cash flow statement)	现金流量表
annual report	年度报告
auditor's report	审计报告
director's report	董事会报告
chairman's statement	董事会声明
corporate governance	公司治理
financial ratio	财务比率
competitor	竞争者
potential investor	潜在投资者
profitability ratio	获利能力比率
return on ordinary shareholders' equity (ROE)	净资产收益率
return on assets (ROA)	资产净利率
profit margin	销售净利率
asset turnover	资产周转率
gross profit margin	销售毛利率
operating expenses to sales ratio	营业费用比率
earnings per share (EPS)	每股收益
price/earnings ratio (P/E ratio)	市盈率
dividend yield ratio	股息收益率
liquidity ratio	短期偿债比率
current ratio	流动比率
quick ratio (acid test ratio)	速动比率
accounts receivable turnover ratio	应收账款周转率
average collection period	应收账款平均收账期
inventory turnover	存货周转率
average days in inventory	存货周转天数

solvency ratio	长期偿债比率
debt to total assets ratio	资产负债率
time interest earned	利息保障倍数
cash debt coverage	现金负债保障比率

Key Concepts

1. Financial statements (or financial reports) are formal records of the financial activities and position of a business, person, or other entities.

2. The purpose of preparing financial statements is to provide users with information which will help them to make better economic decision.

3. Ratios are major tools of financial analysis. A ratio expresses the relationship between various types of financial information.

4. The profitability ratios measure the profit or operating success of an entity for a given period of time.

5. The liquidity ratios measure the short-term ability of an entity to pay its maturing obligations and to meet unexpected need for cash.

6. Solvency ratios measure the ability of an entity to survive over a long period of time.

Extended Reading

财务报表分析的局限性

一、财务报表本身的局限性

财务报表是企业会计系统的产物。每个企业的会计系统，都会受到会计环境和企业会计战略的影响。

会计环境包括会计规范和会计管理、税务与会计的关系、外部审计、会计争端处理的法律系统、资本市场结构、公司治理结构等。这些因素是决定企业会计系统质量的外部因素。会计环境缺陷会导致会计系统缺陷，使之不能完全反映企业的实际状况。会计环境的重要变化会导致会计系统的变化，影响财务数据的可比性。例如，会计规范要求以历史成本报告资产，使财务数据不代表其现行成本或变现价值；会计规范要求假设币值不变，使财务数据不按通货膨胀率或物价水平调整；会计规范要求遵循谨慎性原则，使会计预计损失而不预计收益，有可能少计收益和资产；会计规范要求按年度分期报告，使得会计报表只报告短期信息，不提供反映长期潜力的信息等。

企业会计战略是企业根据环境和经营目标作出的主观选择，不同企业会有不同的会计战略。企业会计战略包括选择会计政策、会计估计、补充披露及报告具体格式。不同的会计战略会导致不同企业的财务报告有所差异，并影响其可比性。例如，对同一会计事项的账务处理，会计准则允许使用几种不同的规则和程序，企业可自行选择，包括存货计价方法、固定资产折旧方法、投资收益确认方法等。虽然财务报表附注对会计政策选择有一定的表述，但报表使用人未必能完成可比性的调整工作。

由于上述两方面的原因，财务报表存在以下三方面的局限性。

(1) 财务报表没有披露企业的全部信息，管理层拥有更多的信息，披露的只是其中一部分。

(2) 已经披露的财务信息存在会计估计误差，不一定是真实情况的准确计量。

(3) 管理层的各项会计政策选择，有可能导致降低可比性。

二、财务报表的可靠性问题

只有根据符合规范的、可靠的财务报表，才能得出正确的分析结论。所谓"符合规范"，是指除了前述三点局限性外，没有更进一步的虚假陈述。外部分析人员很难认定是否存在虚假陈述，财务报表的可靠性问题主要依靠注册会计师鉴证、把关。但是，注册会计师不能保证财务报表没有任何错报和漏报，而且并非所有注册会计师都是尽职尽责的。因此，分析人员必须自己关注财务报表的可靠性，对于可能存在的问题保持足够的警惕。

外部分析人员虽然不能认定是否存在虚假陈述，但是可以发现一些"危险信号"。对于存有危险信号的报表，分析人员要通过更细致的考察或获取其他有关信息，对报表的可靠性作出判断。

常见的危险信号包括如下几种。

(1) 财务报表形式不规范。不规范的财务报表，其可靠性也应受到怀疑。分析人员要注意财务报表是否有遗漏，因为遗漏违背充分披露原则，遗漏可能是因不想讲真话引起；还要注意是否及时提供财务报表，不能及时提供报表暗示企业与注册会计师存在分歧。

(2) 数据反常。反常数据如无合理原因，应考虑该数据的真实性和一贯性是否存在问题。例如，原因不明的会计调整，可能是利用会计政策的灵活性"粉饰"报表；与销售相比应收账款异常增加，可能存在提前确认收入的问题；报表净利润与经营活动产生的现金流量净额的缺口增加，报表利润总额与应纳税所得额之间的缺口增加，可能存在盈余管理问题；大额的资产冲销和第四季度的大额调整，可能是中期报表存在问题，年底受到注册会计师的压力被迫调整。

(3) 大额关联方交易。关联方交易的价格缺乏客观性，会计估计有较大主观性，可能存在转移利润的动机。

(4) 大额资本利得。在经营业绩不佳时，公司可能通过出售长期资产、债转股等交易实现资本利得。

(5) 异常审计报告。无正当理由更换注册会计师，或审计报告附有保留意见，暗示企业财务报表可能"粉饰"过度。

三、比较基础问题

在比较分析时，需要选择比较的参照标准，包括同业数据、本企业历史数据和计划预算数据。

横向比较时需要使用同业标准。同业平均数只有一般性的指导作用，不一定有代表性，不是合理性的标志。选取同行业中一组有代表性的企业求平均数，作为同业标准，可能比整个行业的平均数更有意义。近年来，分析人员更重视以竞争对手的数据作为分析基础。不少公司实行多种经营，没有明确的行业归属，同业比较更加困难。

趋势分析应以本企业历史数据为比较基础。历史数据代表过去，并不代表合理性。经营环境变化后，今年比上年利润提高了，不一定说明已经达到应该达到的水平，甚至不一定说明管理有了改进。会计规范的改变会使财务数据失去直接可比性，要恢复其可比性，成本很高。

实际与计划的差异分析应以预算为比较基础。实际和预算出现差异，可能是执行中有问题，也可能是预算不合理，两者的区分并非易事。

总之，对比较基础本身要准确理解，选择合理的比较对象是进行比较分析的关键，并且要在限定意义上使用分析结论，避免简单化和绝对化。

Questions and Problems

Choose the best answer to the following questions.

1. Which measure is an evaluation of an entity's ability to pay current liabilities?(   )
   A. Quick ratio.　　　　　B. Current ratio.
   C. Both A and B.　　　　D. None of the above.

Introduction to Financial Statements — Chapter 2

2. Which measure is useful in evaluating the efficiency in managing inventories?(　)

A. Inventory turnover.　　B. Average days in inventory.

C. Both A and B.　　D. None of the above.

3. Which of these is not a liquidity ratio?(　)

A. Current ratio.　　B. Asset turnover.

C. Inventory turnover.　　D. Receivable turnover.

4. Silver Fern Limited reported profit $24,000; net sales $400,000; and average assets $600,000 for 2019. What is the 2019 profit margin?(　)

A. 6%　　B. 12%　　C. 40%　　D. 200%

Short answer questions.

1. Which ratios should be used to help answer each of these questions?

(a) How efficient is an entity in using its assets to produce sales?

(b) How long does it take for customers to pay their accounts?

(c) How many dollars of profit were generated for each dollar of sales?

(d) How liquid is this entity?

2. The price/earnings ratio of Domino's Pizza Enterprises Limited was 54.8 and the price/earnings ratio of Telstra Corporation Limited was 16.4. Which company did the securities market favor? Explain.

3. Indicate each of the following changes generally signals good or bad news about an entity:

(a) Decrease in gross margin rate.

(b) Decrease in inventory turnover.

(c) Decrease in quick ratio.

(d) Increase in return on assets.

(e) Increase in price/earnings ratio.

(f) Increase in debt to total assets ratio.

4. Current ratio and quick ratio are both measures of liquidity. Explain how the quick ratio overcome some of the limitations of the current ratio.

Chapter 3
Time Value of Money

Time Value of Money — Chapter 3

Introduction

Please consider this question:

Today, you deposit $10,000 in a bank, which of the following options is better? (assume the annual return is constant)

- You get back $11,000 two years later.
- You get back $5,500 one year later and $5,500 two year later.

As we know a dollar in hand today is worth more than a dollar promised at some time in the future. Because you can deposit the money and earn interest; inflation makes next year's $1 less valuable than today's or the uncertainty of receiving next year's $1. These factors will all change the value of money as time goes on. Therefore, when we make financial decisions, we must take time and money into consideration.

3.1 Value Creation and Corporate Investment

If we accept that the objective of investment within a firm is to create value for its owners, then the purpose of allocating money to a particular division or project is to generate cash inflows in the future significantly greater than the amount invested, then put most simply, the project appraisal decision is one involving the comparison of the amount of cash put into an investment with the amount of cash returned. The key phrase and the tricky issue is "significantly greater than". For instance, would you, as part-owner of a firm, be content if the firm asked you to swap $10,000 of your hard-earned money for some new shares so that the management team could invest it in order to hand it back to you, in five years, plus $1,000? Is this a significant return? Would you feel that your wealth had been enhanced if you were aware that by investing the $10,000 yourself, for instance, lending to the government, you could have received a 5 percent return per year? Or that you could obtain a return of 10 percent per annum by investing in other shares on the stock market? Naturally, you would feel let down by a management team that offered a return of less than 2 percent per year when you had alternative courses of action that would have produced much more.

This line of thought is leading us to a central concept in finance and, indeed, in business generally — the time value of money. Investors have alternative uses for their funds and they therefore have an opportunity cost if money is invested in a corporate project. The investor's opportunity cost is the sacrifice of the return available on the best forgone alternative.

Investments must generate at least enough cash for all investors to obtain their required returns. If they produce less than the investor's opportunity cost, then the wealth of shareholders will decline.

3.2 Simple and Compound Interest

When there are time delays between receipts and payments of financial sums, we need to make use of the concepts of simple and compound interest.

3.2.1 Simple Interest

Simple interest is the interest that is paid only on the original principal. No interest is paid on the accumulated interest payments.

Example 3-1

Suppose that a sum of $10 is deposited in a bank account that pays 12 percent annum. At the end of year 1, the investor would have $11.20 in the account. That is:

$$F = P(1+i)$$
$$\$11.20 = 10 \times (1+0.12)$$

Where F = Future value, P = Present value, i = Interest rate.

The initial sum, called the principal, is multiplied by the interest rate to give the annual return. At the end of five years:

$$F = P(1+i \cdot n)$$

Where n = number of years. Thus,

$$\$16 = 10 \times (1+0.12 \times 5)$$

Note from the Example 3-1 that the 12 percent return is a constant amount each year. Interest is not earned on the interest already accumulated from the previous years.

3.2.2 Compound Interest

The more usual situation in the real world is for interest to be paid on the sum that accumulates—whether or not that sum comes from the principal or from the interest received in previous periods.

Example 3-2

An investment of $10 is made at an interest rate of 12 percent with the interest being compounded. In one year the capital would grow by 12 percent to $11.20. In the second year the capital would grow by 12 percent, but this time the growth would be on the accumulated

value of $11.20 and thus would amount to an extra $1.34. At the end of two years:
$$F = P(1+i)(1+i)$$
$$F = 11.20(1+0.12) = \$12.54$$

Alternatively,
$$F = P(1+i)^2$$

Over five years the result would be:
$$F = P(1+i)^5$$
$$\$17.62 = 10 \times (1+0.12)^5$$

The interest on the accumulated interest was therefore the difference between the total arising from simple interest and that from the compound interest:
$$17.62 - 16.00 = \$1.62$$

Almost all investments pay compound interest, so we will be using compounding throughout the book.

3.3 Future Value and Present Value

3.3.1 Future Value

Future value measures the nominal future sum of money that a given sum of money is "worth" at a specified time in the future assuming a certain interest rate, or more generally, rate of return; it is the present value multiplied by the accumulation function. The formula can be seen from Example 3-2.

Also, discount factors can be used, as shown in Table 3-1 (this is an extract from Appendix I at the end of the book). Table 3-1 displays the future value of $1 invested at a number of different compound interest rates and for alternative numbers of years.

Table 3-1 Future value of $1 at compound interest

Year	Interest rate (per annum)				
	1%	5%	10%	12%	15%
1	1.0100	1.0500	1.1000	1.1200	1.1500
2	1.0201	1.1025	1.2100	1.2544	1.3225
3	1.0303	1.1576	1.3310	1.4049	1.5209
4	1.0406	1.2155	1.4641	1.5735	1.7490
5	1.0510	1.2763	1.6105	1.7623	2.0114

From the fourth column of the table in Table 3-1 we can read that $1 invested for two years at 12 percent amounts to $1.2544. Thus, the investment of $10 provides a future capital sum 1.2544 times the original amount:

$$10 \times 1.2544 = \$12.544$$

3.3.2 Present Value

There are many occasions in financial management when you are given the future sums and need to find out what those future sums are worth in present value terms today. For example, you wish to know how much you would have to put aside today which will accumulate, with compounded interest, to a defined sum in the future; or you are given the choice between receiving $200 in five years or $100 now and wish to know which is the better option, given anticipated interest rates; or a project gives a return of $1,000,000 in three years for an outlay of $800,000 now and you need to establish if this is the best use of the $800,000. By the process of discounting, a sum of money to be received in the future is given a monetary value today.

Example 3-3

If we anticipate the receipt of $17.62 in five years' time we can determine its present value. Rearrangement of the compound formula, and assuming a discount rate of 12 percent, gives:

$$P = \frac{F}{(1+i)^n}$$

$$\$10 = \frac{17.62}{(1+0.12)^5}$$

Alternatively, discount factors may be used, as shown in Table 3-2 (this is an extract from Appendix II at the end of the book). The factor needed to discount 1 receivable in five years when the discount rate is 12 percent is 0.5674.

Therefore the present value of $17.62 is:

$$0.5674 \times 17.62 = \$10$$

Examining the present value table in Table 3-2 you can see that, as the discount rate increases, the present value goes down.

Table 3-2 Present value of $1 at compound interest

Year	Interest rate (per annum)				
	1%	5%	10%	12%	15%
1	0.9901	0.9524	0.9091	0.8929	0.8696
2	0.9803	0.9070	0.8264	0.7972	0.7561
3	0.9706	0.8638	0.7513	0.7118	0.6575
4	0.9610	0.8227	0.6830	0.6355	0.5718
5	0.9515	0.7835	0.6209	0.5674	0.4972

3.3.3 Determining the Rate of Interest

Sometimes you want to calculate the rate of return that a project is earning. For instance, a savings company may offer to pay you $10,000 in five years if you deposit $8,000 now, when interest rates on accounts elsewhere are offering 6 percent per annum. In order to make a comparison you need to know the annual rate being offered by the savings company. Thus, we need to find i in the discounting equation.

To be able to calculate i, it is necessary to rearrange the compounding formula.

$$F = P(1+i)^n$$

Therefore,

$$i = \sqrt[n]{F/P} - 1$$

Alternatively, use the future value table, an extract of which is shown in Table 3-2. In our example, the return on $1 worth of investment over five years is:

$$17.62/10 = \$1.762$$

In the body of the future value table, look at the year 5 row for a future value of $1.762, read off the interest rate of 12 percent.

3.3.4 Annuity

Quite often there is not just one payment at the end of a certain number of years. There can be a series of identical payments made over a period of years. For instance:

● Bonds usually pay a regular rate of interest;

● Individuals can buy, from saving plan companies, the right to receive a number of identical payments over a number of years;

● A business may invest in a project which, it is estimated, will give regular cash inflows over a period of years.

An annuity is a series of payments or receipts of equal amounts. We are able to calculate the present value and future value of this set of payments.

Annuities are usually classified into four categories:

● **Ordinary annuity**— is an annuity whose payments are made at the end of each period.

● **Annuity due**— is an annuity whose payments are made at the beginning of each period.

● **Deferred annuity**— is an annuity in which the first cash flow in the series occurs beyond one period from today.

- **Perpetuity**— is an annuity for which the payments continue forever.

1. Ordinary Annuity

(1) Future Value of an Ordinary Annuity

Example 3-4

For a regular payment of $10 per year for five years, when the interest rate is 12 percent, we can calculate the future value of the annuity by three methods.

Method 1:

$$F_A = A + A(1+i) + A(1+i)^2 + A(1+i)^3 + A(1+i)^4$$

where A = the periodic receipt.

$$F_A = 10 + 10(1+0.12) + 10(1+0.12)^2 + 10(1+0.12)^3 + 10(1+0.12)^4 = \$63.53$$

Method 2:

Using the derived formula:

$$F_A = \frac{(1+i)^n - 1}{i} \times A$$

$$F_A = \frac{(1+0.12)^5 - 1}{i} \times 10 = \$63.53$$

Method 3:

Use the "future value of an annuity" table. (See Table 3-3, an extract from the more complete annuity table at the end of the book in Appendix III.) Here we simply look along the year 5 row and 12 percent column to find the figure of 6.3528. This refers to the future value of five annual receipts of $1. Therefore we multiply by $10:

$$6.3528 \times 10 \approx \$63.53$$

Table 3-3 The future value of an annuity of $1 at compound interest

Year	Interest rate (per annum)				
	1%	5%	10%	12%	15%
1	1.0000	1.0000	1.0000	1.0000	1.0000
2	2.0100	2.0500	2.1000	2.1200	2.1500
3	3.0301	3.1525	3.3100	3.3744	3.4725
4	4.0604	4.3101	4.6410	4.7793	4.9934
5	5.1010	5.5256	6.1051	6.3528	6.7424

(2) Present Value of an Ordinary Annuity

Example 3-5

For a regular payment of $10 per year for five years, when the interest rate is 12 percent, we can calculate the present value of the annuity by three methods.

Method 1:

$$P_A = \frac{A}{(1+i)} + \frac{A}{(1+i)^2} + \frac{A}{(1+i)^3} + \frac{A}{(1+i)^4} + \frac{A}{(1+i)^5}$$

where A = the periodic receipt.

$$P_A = \frac{10}{(1+0.12)} + \frac{10}{(1+0.12)^2} + \frac{10}{(1+0.12)^3} + \frac{10}{(1+0.12)^4} + \frac{10}{(1+0.12)^5} = \$36.05$$

Method 2:

Using the derived formula:

$$P_A = \frac{1 - 1/(1+i)^n}{i} \times A$$

$$P_A = \frac{1 - 1/(1+0.12)^5}{0.12} \times 10 = \$36.05$$

Method 3:

Use the "present value of an annuity" table. (See Table 3-4, an extract from the more complete annuity table at the end of the book in Appendix IV.) Here we simply look along the year 5 row and 12 percent column to find the figure of 3.6048. This refers to the present value of five annual receipts of $1. Therefore we multiply by $10:

$$3.6046 \times 10 \approx \$36.05$$

Table 3-4 The present value of an annuity of $1 at compound interest

Year	Interest rate (per annum)				
	1%	5%	10%	12%	15%
1	0.9901	0.9524	0.9091	0.8929	0.8696
2	1.9704	1.8594	1.7355	1.6901	1.6257
3	2.9410	2.7232	2.4869	2.4018	2.2832
4	3.9020	3.5460	3.1699	3.0373	2.8550
5	4.8534	4.3295	3.7908	3.6048	3.3522

2. Annuity Due

The distinguishing factor with an annuity due is the fact that the first cash flow occurs on the valuation date, i.e., immediately. Thus the only material difference between an ordinary annuity and an annuity due is the timing of the cash flow.

The natural solution to this difference is to reduce the annuity period by one, since the first cash flow is already in its present value form, i.e., it is paid immediately and thus requires no further discounting. Therefore, the correct adjustment for an annuity due is to reduce the discounting factor by one and to add to the reduced calculation a non-discounted cash flow stream.

For instance, if we use Example 3-4 and Example 3-5 as an example, but just change the payment time from the end of each period to the beginning of each period, then the formula of present value and future value will be:

a. Present Value of an Annuity Due

$$P_A = \frac{A}{(1+i)} + \frac{A}{(1+i)^2} + \frac{A}{(1+i)^3} + \frac{A}{(1+i)^4}$$

or
$$P_A = \frac{1-1/(1+i)^n}{i} \times A \times (1+i)$$

b. Future Value of an Annuity Due

$$F_A = A(1+i) + A(1+i)^2 + A(1+i)^3 + A(1+i)^4 + A(1+i)^5$$

or
$$F_A = \frac{(1+i)^n - 1}{i} \times A \times (1+i)$$

3. Deferred Annuity

If an annuity does not begin its payment in the first period, as with an ordinary annuity, or immediately, as with an annuity due, then it is classified as a deferred annuity — an annuity that begins its cash flow stream subsequent to the first period. A common example is superannuation. With this form of investment, cash flow is added, but no periodic cash outflow is exhibited for a number of years until retirement.

A simple two-stage discounting method is applied that combines the techniques employed above. Essentially, the periodic payments are discounted back to the first period prior to the beginning of the cash flow stream. This value is then discounted back to time zero.

a. Present Value of Deferred Annuity (assume m is the interval period before the annuity begins its cash flow)

$$P_A = A \times (P_A/A, i, n) \times (P/F, i, m)$$

or
$$P_A = A \times [(P_A/A, i, m+n) - (P_A/A, i, m)]$$

b. Future Value of Deferred Annuity

$$F_A = A \times (F_A/A, i, n)$$

4. Perpetuity

Some contracts run in definitely and there is no end to the series of payments. Perpetuities are rare in the private sector, but certain government securities do not have an end date; that is, the amount paid when the bond was purchased by the lender will never be repaid, only interest payments are made. The value of a perpetuity is simply the annual amount received divided by the interest rate when the latter is expressed as a decimal.

$$P_A = \frac{A}{i}$$

If $10 is to be received as an indefinite annual payment then the present value, at a discount rate of 12 percent, is:

$$P_A = \frac{10}{0.12} = \$83.33$$

It is very important to note that in order to use this formula. we are assuming that the first payment arises 365 days after the time at which we are standing (the present time or time zero).

Core Words

time value of money	货币时间价值
simple interest	单利
compound interest	复利
future value	终值
present value	现值
principal	本金
terminal value	终值
discounting	折现计算
discount rate	折现率
required rate of return	要求报酬率
annuity	年金
ordinary annuity	普通年金
annuity due	预付年金
deferred annuity	递延年金
perpetuity	永续年金

Key Concepts

1. The time value of money states that the value of money you have now is greater than a reliable promise to receive the same amount of money at a future date.

2. Simple interest is the interest that is paid only on the original principal. No interest is paid on the accumulated interest payments.

3. Compound interest is the addition of interest to the principal sum of a loan or deposit,

or in other words, interest on interest.

4. Future value: $F = P(1+i)^n$

5. Present value: $P = \dfrac{F}{(1+i)^n}$

6. Future value of an ordinary annuity: $F_A = \dfrac{(1+i)^n - 1}{i} \times A$

Present value of an ordinary annuity: $P_A = \dfrac{1 - 1/(1+i)^n}{i} \times A$

7. Future value of an annuity due: $F_A = \dfrac{(1+i)^n - 1}{i} \times A \times (1+i)$

Present value of an annuity due: $P_A = \dfrac{1 - 1/(1+i)^n}{i} \times A \times (1+i)$

8. Present value of deferred annuity (assume m is the interval period before the annuity begins its cash flow): $P_A = A \times (P_A/A, i, n) \times (P/F, i, m)$

or $\qquad P_A = A \times [(P_A/A, i, m+n) - (P_A/A, i, m)]$

Future value of deferred annuity: $F_A = A \times (F_A/A, i, n)$

9. Present value of perpetuity: $P_A = \dfrac{A}{i}$

Extended Reading

按揭贷款中的货币时间价值

货币的时间价值，是指货币经历一定时间的投资和再投资所增加的价值，只要时间不止，货币的时间价值就会生生不息。货币时间价值在现实生活中有非常广泛的应用。货币时间价值的计量有两种方法：一种是单利法，另一种是复利法。按揭贷款的一个显著特点就是分期偿还本金和利息，利息属于货币时间价值的内容。假如某人买房向银行按揭贷款50万元，历时10年还清，每月等额还款，每月支付5,525.95元，10年一共支付663,113.94元，多出来的163,113.94元就是按揭贷款占用银行50万元资金所支付的货币时间价值。

目前按揭贷款中商业银行普遍采用的还款方式有两种：等额本息还款法和等额本金还款法。等额本息还款法是指在整个还款期内，每个月还款额相等，每个月的还款额包括本金和利息，但是每个月支付的本金和利息并不相等，是用复利法计算利息。等额本金还款法，顾名思义，每个月偿还相同金额的本金和剩余贷款在本月产生的利息，是用单利法计算利息。由于剩余贷款随着还款时间的增加会减少，因此等额本金还款法每个月还的本金不变，利息递减，前期每个月还款金额多，后期少。

假设你准备按揭贷款400,000元购买一套房子，贷款期限20年，年利率为6%，每月末偿还一次。

(1) 若选择等额本息法还款，贷款月利率=0.06/12=0.005，复利计算期为240期，则

$$按揭贷款月支付额 = 400,000 \times \left[\frac{0.06/12}{1-(1+0.06/12)^{-240}}\right] = 2,866(元)$$

年末	分期付款 (1)	每期利息 $(2)=(4)_{t-1} \times 0.005$	偿还本金 $(3)=(1)-(2)$	期末未还本金 $(4)=(4)_{t-1}-(3)$
0				400,000.00
1	2,865.72	2,000.00	865.72	399,134.28
2	2,865.72	1,995.67	870.05	398,264.22
3	2,865.72	1,991.32	874.40	397,389.82
4	2,865.72	1,986.95	878.78	396,511.04
5	2,865.72	1,982.56	883.17	395,627.88
...	...	...	...	...
240	2,865.72	14.26		0
合计	687,773.82	287,773.82	400,000.00	

上述计算表明，每月支付2,866元就能在20年内偿付400,000元，每期付款额是由利息和本金两部分组成。

(2) 若选择等额本金法，则

$$每期本金 = 400,000 \div 240 = 1,666.67(元)$$

年末	每期本金 (1)	每期利息 $(2)=(4)_{t-1} \times 0.005$	偿还本息 $(3)=(1)+(2)$	期末未还本金 $(4)=(4)_{t-1}-(1)$
0				400,000.00
1	1,666.67	2,000.00	3,666.67	398,333.33
2	1,666.67	1,991.67	3,658.33	396,666.67
3	1,666.67	1,983.33	3,650.00	395,000.00
4	1,666.67	1,975.00	3,641.67	393,333.33
5	1,666.67	1,966.67	3,633.33	391,666.67
...	...	...	...	...
240	1,666.67	8.33	1,675.00	0
合计	400,000.00	241,000.00	641,000.00	

Questions and Problems

Numerical problems.

1. You plan to invest $10,000 in the shares of a company.

    a. If the value of the shares increases by 5 percent a year, what will be the value of the shares in 20 years?

    b. If the value of the shares increases by 15 percent a year, what will be the value of the shares in 20 years?

2. As a winner of a lottery, you can choose one of the following prizes:

    a. $1,000,000 now.

    b. $1,700,000 at the end of 5 years.

    c. $135,000 a year for ever, starting in year 1.

    d. $200,000 for each of the next 10 years, starting in year 1.

    If the time value of money is 9 percent, which is the most valuable prize?

3. A bank lends a customer $5,000. At the end of 10 years he repays this amount plus interest. The amount he repays is $8,950. What is the rate of interest charged by the bank?

4. Peter plc is considering two investment projects whose cash flows are:

Points in time (yearly intervals)	Project A	Project B
0	$ − 120,000	$ − 120,000
1	60,000	15,000
2	45,000	45,000
3	42,000	55,000
4	18,000	60,000

The company's required rate of return is 15 percent. What are the present value for these two projects?

5. Punter buys a car on hire purchases paying five annual installments of $1,500, the first being an immediate cash deposit. Assuming an interest rate of 8 percent is being charged by the hire purchase company, how much is the current cash price of the car?

6. How much must be invested now to provide an amount of $10,000 in six years' time assuming interest is compounded quarterly at a nominal annual rate of 8 percent? What is the effective annual rate?

Part II
Capital Budgeting

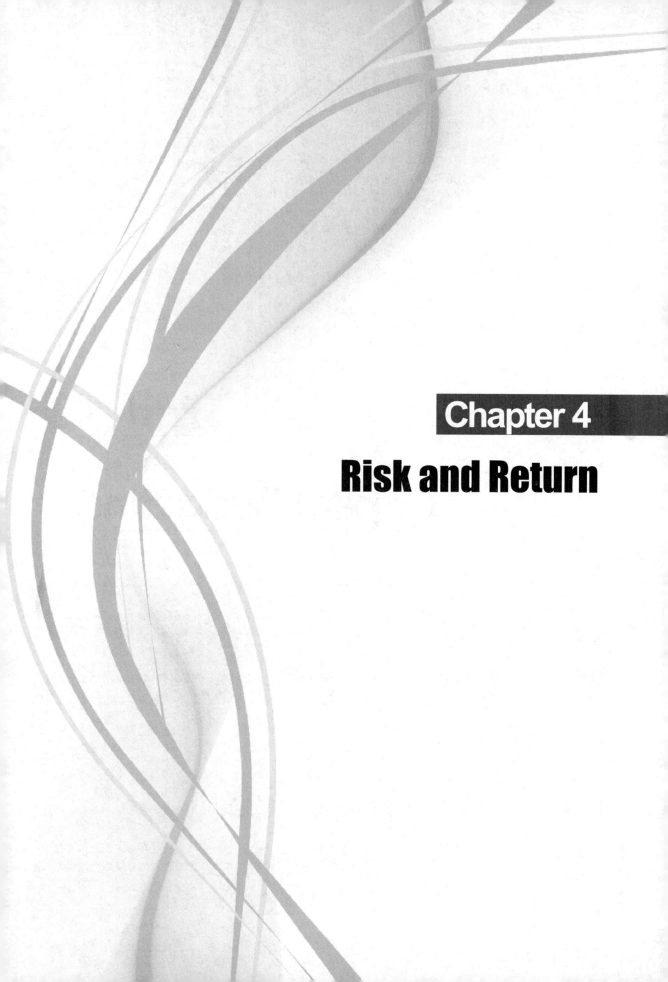

Chapter 4

Risk and Return

Introduction

Every day we make decisions that involve financial or economic risk. How much car insurance should we buy? Should we refinance the mortgage now or a year from now? Should we buy a lottery ticket in view of potential returns of hundreds or thousands of dollars? Making any decision that has more than one possible outcome is similar to gambling: we put the money on the roulette table and take our chances.

Most people view risk as a curse to be avoided whenever possible, while risk also creates opportunities. When we buy insurance, we pay someone else to take our risks, so it makes sense that if someone wants us to take on a risk, we need to be paid to do it. A risky investment, then, must have an expected return that is higher than the return on a risk-free asset. In economic terms, it must offer a risk premium. By extension, if riskier investments have higher risk premiums, they must have higher expected returns. Thus, there is a trade-off between risk and expected return; you can not get high return without taking considerable risks. So if someone tells you he or she made a big return on a investment, you should suspect that it was a very risky investment. No risk, no reward!

This chapter review makes use of many of the statistical and returns measures we covered in quantitative methods. We should understand the historical return and risk rankings of the major asset classes and how the correlation of returns between assets and between various asset classes affect the risk of portfolios. Then we should describe an investor's preference related to the tradeoff between risk and return. These preferences, along with the risk and return characteristics of available portfolios, can be used to illustrate the selection of optimal for a given investor, that is, the portfolio that maximizes the investor's expected utility.

4.1 Understanding Return

4.1.1 Return

A return expresses the financial performance of a financial asset (or investment), which might be above or below its value at the time of purchase/investment. You can think of it as the "pay-off" to your investment. A return can be expressed in either monetary ($) or percentage(%) terms and essentially shows the difference between the initial purchase/investment cost and the market value at some later point. Returns to financial asset or investment can be calculated over any time period, annually, quarterly or even daily.

4.1.2 Measuring Return

1. Total Return

Any measurement of past return includes both the impact of capital gains (or losses) and income received over a holding period. This total return is computed as:

$$Total\ return = \frac{Ending\ price - Beginning\ price + Income}{Beginning\ price}$$

2. Average Return

The arithmetic mean return is the simple average of the series of periodic returns. It has the statistical property of being an unbiased estimator of the true mean of the underlying distribution of returns:

$$Arithmetic\ mean\ return = \frac{R_1 + R_2 + R_3 + \cdots + R_n}{n}$$

3. Expected Return

In financial management, we often need to measure the average reward that you expect to receive from making an investment. Usually, we use the expected return of the investment as our measure. The expected return is the probability-weighted average of all possible returns, which is one of the most important financial management concepts. To denote the expected value, use the notion E. The expected return formula is:

$$E(R) = \sum_{i=1}^{n} R_i P_i$$

Where: R_i = possible returns;

P_i = the probability of possible returns.

4.2 Understanding Risk

4.2.1 Risk

1. Defining Risk

The dictionary definition of risk, the "possibility of loss or injury", focuses on the perils of putting oneself in a situation in which the outcome is unknown. But this common use of the word doesn't quite fit our purposes because we care about gains as well as losses. We need a definition of risk that focuses on the fact that outcomes of financial and economic decisions are almost always unknown at the time the decisions are made. Here is the definition we will use:

Risk is a measure of uncertainty about the future payoff on an investment, measured over some time horizon and relative to a benchmark.

2. Classifying Risks

Risk is everywhere. It comes in many forms and from almost every imaginable place. We can classify all risks into one of two groups:①those affecting a small number of people but no one else and②those affecting everyone. We will call the first of these idiosyncratic or diversifiable risk and the second systematic or market risk.

3. Risk Preference

We often assume that everyone is risk-neutral, but investors truly are risk-averse in the real world. Choosing investments on the basis of expected return is assuming risk-neutrality. Only for learning purposes, we often assume that everyone is risk-neutral. Essentially, this means that investors are willing to take any fair risky investment.

In fact, we should judge all opportunities not only for their reward, but also by their risk. Risk aversion means you would prefer the safe project, so you would demand an extra risk reward to take the riskier project. For an investor, bigger risk usually requires more compensation. But financial markets can spread risk, and thereby lower the aggregate risk aversion. If you are risk-averse, you would not invest in the riskier alternative investment when both the risky and safe alternative investment offered the same expected return.

4.2.2 Measuring Risk

In finance, the variance and standard deviation of returns are common measures of investment risk. Both of these are measures of variability of a distribution of returns about its mean or expected value.

We can calculate the population variance, σ^2, when we know the return R for each period, the total number periods (T), and the mean or expected value of the population's distribution (μ), as follows:

$$\sigma^2 = \frac{\sum_{t=1}^{T}(R_t - \mu)^2}{T}$$

4.3 Portfolio Theory

4.3.1 Basic Assumptions

In financial management there is a trade-off between the risk associated with an investment and financial return that it offers. The risk-return relationship is a positive one because the more risk that is assumed, the higher the required rate of return. Knowing how to build an investment portfolio effectively is the most important challenge for investors. A well-designed investment portfolio combines stocks, bonds, real estate, and other investments in such a way as to achieve an efficient trade-off between risk and expected return. Portfolio theory is the simple concept of making security choices based on the expected return and risk of a collection of securities.

Investors like more return and less risk. The diversification of an investment portfolio can reduce risk. An intuitive explanation of this investment diversification is based on the proverb: do not put all your eggs into one basket. The volatility can be calculated equally well for individual securities and a portfolio of securities. The market portfolio is made up of individual stocks, but its volatility doesn't reflect the average volatility of its components in that diversification of an investment portfolio reduces volatility. Even a little diversification can provide a substantial reduction in volatility.

Modern portfolio theory (MPT), or mean-variance analysis, is a mathematical framework for assembling a portfolio of assets that the expected return is maximized for a given level of risk, defined as variance. Its key insight is that an asset's risk and return should not be assessed by itself, but by how it contributes to a portfolio's overall risk and return.

4.3.2 Portfolio Return and Risk

1. Portfolio Return

We will learn how to compute the return of a portfolio of assets. Let's start with a two assets portfolio.

Let's say the returns from the two assets in the portfolio are R_1 and R_2. Also, assume the weights of the two assets in the portfolio are w_1 and w_2. Note that the sum of the weights of the assets in the portfolio should be 1. The returns from the portfolio will simply be the weighted average of the returns from the two assets, as shown below:

$$R_p = W_1 R_1 + W_2 R_2$$

Let's take a simple example. You invested $60,000 in asset 1 that produced 20% returns and $40,000 in asset 2 that produced 12% returns. The weights of the two assets are 60% and 40% respectively.

The portfolio return will be:
$$R_p = 0.60 \times 20\% + 0.40 \times 12\% = 16.8\%$$

Thus the portfolio return can be calculated as follows:
$$R_p = \sum_{i=1}^{n} w_i R_i$$

Where: R_p is the return of the portfolio; W_i is the proportion of the portfolio invested in asset i; R_i is the return of the asset i.

The expected return of portfolio formula is:
$$E(R_p) = \sum_{i=1}^{n} w_i E(R_i)$$

Where: $E(R_p)$ is the expected return of the portfolio; W_i is the proportion of the portfolio invested in asset i; $E(R_i)$ is the expected return of the asset i.

2. Portfolio Risk

Let's now look at how to calculate the risk of the portfolio. The risk of a portfolio is measured using the standard deviation of the portfolio. However, the standard deviation of the portfolio will not be simply the weighted average of the standard deviation of the two assets. We also need to consider the covariance/correlation between the assets. The covariance reflects the co-movement of the returns of the two assets. Unless the two assets are perfectly correlated, the covariance will have the impact of reduction in the overall risk of the portfolio.

The portfolio standard deviation can be calculated as follows:
$$\text{Var}_p = w_1^2 \sigma_1^2 + w_2^2 \sigma_2^2 + 2 w_1 w_2 \text{COV}_{1,2}$$
$$\text{Var}_p = w_1^2 \sigma_1^2 + w_2^2 \sigma_2^2 + 2 w_1 w_2 \rho_{1,2} \sigma_1 \sigma_2$$
$$\sigma_p = \sqrt{\text{Var}_p}$$

Where: Var_p is the variance of returns for a portfolio of two assets; w_1 is the proportion of the portfolio invested in asset 1; w_2 is the proportion of the portfolio invested in asset 2; $w_1+w_2=1$.

Thus, the standard deviation of a portfolio is calculated using the expression
$$\text{Var}(R_p) = \sum_{i=1}^{n} w_i^2 \text{Var}(R_i) + \sum_{i=1}^{n}\sum_{j=1}^{n} w_i w_j \text{COV}(R_i R_j) \quad (i \neq j)$$
$$\sigma_p = \sqrt{\text{Var}(R_p)}$$

Where: $\text{Var}(R_p)$ is the variance of returns for a portfolio of n assets; w_i is the proportion of the portfolio invested in asset i; w_j is the proportion of the portfolio invested in asset j.

3. Covariance and Correlation of Returns for Two Assets

Covariance measures the extent to which two variables move together over time. A positive covariance means that the two variables tend to move together. Negative covariance means that the two variables tend to move in opposite directions. A covariance of zero means there is no linear relationship between the two variables. To put is another way, if the covariance or return between two assets is zero, knowing the return for the next period on one of the assets tells you nothing about the return of the other asset for the period.

Here we will focus on the calculation of the covariance between two assets' returns using historical data. The calculation of the sample covariance is based on the following formula:

$$COV_{1,2} = \frac{\sum_{t=1}^{n}\{R_{t,1}-\overline{R}_1 | R_{t,2}-\overline{R}_2\}}{n-1}$$

Where: $R_{t,1}$= return an asset 1 in period t;

$R_{t,2}$= return an asset 2 in period t;

R_1= mean return an asset 1;

R_2= mean return an asset 2;

n = number of period.

The magnitude of the covariance depends on the magnitude of the individual stock's standard deviations and the relation between their co-movements. Covariance is an absolute measure and is measured in return units squared.

The covariance of the returns of two assets can be standardized by dividing by the product of the standard deviations of the two assets. This standardized measure of co-movement is called correlation as:

$$\rho_{1,2} = \frac{COV_{1,2}}{\sigma_1\sigma_2}$$

The relation can also be written as:

$$COV_{1,2} = \rho_{1,2}\sigma_1\sigma_2$$

The term $\rho_{1,2}$ is called the correlation coefficient between the returns of assets 1 and 2. The correlation coefficient has no units. It is a pure measure of the co-movement of the two assets' returns and is bounded by -1 and $+1$.

Interpret the correlation coefficient:

(1) A correlation coefficient of $+1$ means that deviations from the mean or expected return

are always proportional in the same direction. That is, they are perfectly positively correlated.

(2) A correlation coefficient of −1 means that deviations from the mean or expected return are always proportional in opposite directions. That is, they are perfectly negatively correlated.

(3) A correlation coefficient of zero means that there is no linear relationship between the two assets' returns. They are uncorrelated. One way to interpret a correlation of 0 is that, in any period, knowing the actual value of one variable tells you nothing about the value of the other.

4. The Effect on a Portfolio's Risk of Investing in Assets of Different Correlation Coefficient

If two risky assets' returns are perfectly positively correlated, $\rho_{1,2} = +1$, then the square root of portfolio variance is equal to

$$\sigma_p = \sqrt{w_1^2 \sigma_1^2 + w_2^2 \sigma_2^2 + 2w_2 \sigma_1 \sigma_2} = w_1 \sigma_1 + w_2 \sigma_2$$

Focusing on the returns correlation, we can see that the greatest portfolio risk results when the correlation between assets' returns is +1. For any value of correlation less than +1, portfolio variance is reduced. Note that for a correlation of 0, the entire third term in the portfolio variance equation is 0. For negative values of correlation $\rho_{1,2}$, the third term becomes negative and further reduced portfolio variance and standard deviation.

Example 4-1

Consider two risky assets that have returns variance of 0.0625 and 0.0324, respectively. The assets' standard deviation of returns are then 25% and 18%, respectively.

Calculate the variances and standard deviation of portfolio returns for an equal weighted portfolio of the two assets when their correlation of return is 1, 0.5, 0, −0.5.

Answer:

$$\text{Var}_p = w_1^2 \sigma_1^2 + w_2^2 \sigma_2^2 + 2w_1 w_2 \rho_{1,2} \sigma_1 \sigma_2$$

$$\sigma_p = \sqrt{\text{Var}_p}$$

$\rho = 1$

$\sigma^2 = 0.215^2 = 0.046,225$

$\sigma = 0.5 \times 25\% + 0.5 \times 18\% = 21.5\%$

$\rho = 0.5$

$\sigma^2 = 0.5^2 \times 0.062,5 + 0.5^2 \times 0.032,4 + 2 \times 0.5 \times 0.5 \times 0.25 \times 0.18 = 0.034,975$

$\sigma = 18.7\%$

$\rho = 0$

$\sigma^2 = 0.52 \times 0.062,5 + 0.52 \times 0.032,4 = 0.023,725$

$\sigma = 15.4\%$

$\rho = -0.5$

$\sigma^2 = 0.52 \times 0.062,5 + 0.52 \times 0.032,4 - 2 \times 0.5 \times 0.5 \times 0.25 \times 0.18 = 0.012,475$

$\sigma = 11.17\%$

Note that portfolio risk falls as the correlation between the assets' returns decreases. This is an important result of the analysis of portfolio risk: the lower the correlation of asset returns, the greater the risk reduction (diversification) benefits of combining assets in a portfolio. If asset returns were perfectly negatively correlated, portfolio risk could be eliminated altogether for a specific of asset weights.

We show these relations graphically in Figure 4-1 by plotting the portfolio risk and return for all portfolio of two risky assets, for assumed values of the assets' returns correlation.

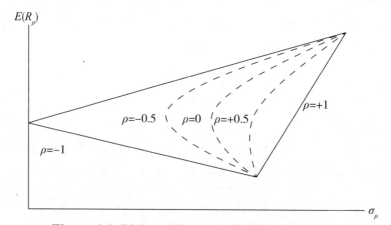

Figure 4-1 Risk and Return of Different Values

4.3.3 Minimum-Variance and Efficient Frontiers

For each level of expected portfolio return, we can vary the portfolio weights on the individual assets to determine the portfolio that has the least risk. These portfolios that have the lowest standard deviation of all portfolios with a given expected return are known as minimum-variance portfolios. Together they make up the minimum-variance frontier. On a risk versus return graph, the portfolio that is farthest to the left (has the least risk) is known as the global minimum-variance portfolio.

Assuming that investors are risk averse, investors prefer the portfolio that has the greatest expected return when choosing among portfolios that have the same standard deviation of returns. Those portfolios that have the greatest expected return for each level of risk (standard deviation) make up the efficient frontier. The efficient frontier coincides with the top portion of the minimum-variance frontier. A risk-averse investor would only choose portfolios that are on the efficient frontier because all available portfolios that are not on the efficient frontier have lower expected returns than an efficient portfolio with the same risk. The portfolio on the efficient frontier that has the least risk is the global minimum-variance portfolio.

These concepts are illustrated in Figure 4-2.

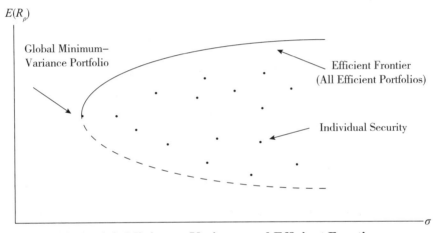

Figure 4-2 Minimum-Variance and Efficient Frontiers

4.3.4 The Selection of an Optimal Portfolio

An investor's utility function represents the investor's preferences in terms of risk and return (i.e., his degree of risk aversion). An indifference curve is a tool from economics that, in this application, plots combinations of risk (standard deviation) and expected return among which an investor is indifferent. In constructing indifference curves for portfolios based on only their expected return and standard deviation of returns, we are assuming that these are the only portfolio characteristics that investors care about.

In Figure 4-3, we show three indifference curves for an investor. The investor's expected utility is the same for all points along a single indifference curve. Indifference curve I_1 represents the most preferred portfolio in Figure 4-3; our investor will prefer any portfolio along I_1 to any portfolio on either I_2 or I_3.

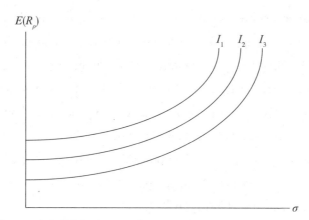

Figure 4-3 Risk-Averse Investor's Indifference Curves

Indifference curves slope upward for risk-averse investors because they will only take on more risk (standard deviation of returns) if they are compensated with greater expected returns. An investor who is relatively more risk averse requires a relatively greater increase in expected return to compensate for a given increase in risk. In other words, a more risk-averse investor will have steeper indifference curves.

In our previous illustration of efficient portfolios available in the market, we included only risky assets. Now we will introduce a risk-free asset into our universe of available assets, and we will consider the risk and return characteristics of a portfolio that combines a portfolio of risky asset and the risk-free asset. Recall from Quantitative Methods that we can calculate the expected return and standard deviation of a portfolio with weight W_A allocated to risky Asset A and weight W_B allocated to risky Asset B using the following formulas:

$$E(R_p) = W_A E(R_A) + W_B E(R_B)$$
$$\text{Var}_p = W_A^2 \sigma_A^2 + W_B^2 \sigma_B^2 + 2 W_A W_B \rho_{A,B} \sigma_A \sigma_B$$

Allow Asset B to be the risk-free asset and Asset A to be the risky asset portfolio. Because a risk-free asset has zero standard deviation and zero correlation of returns with those of a risky portfolio, this results in the reduced equation:

$$\sigma_p = \sqrt{w_A^2 \sigma_A^2} = w_A \sigma_A$$

The intuition of this result is quite simple. If we put $X\%$ of our portfolio into the risky asset portfolio, the resulting portfolio will have a standard deviation of returns equal to $X\%$ of the standard deviation of the risky asset portfolio. The relationship between portfolio risk and return for various portfolio allocations is linear, as illustrated in Figure 4-4.

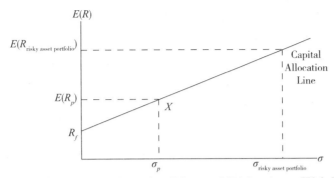

Figure 4-4 Capital Allocation Line and Risky Asset Weights

Combining a risky portfolio with a risk-free asset is the process that supports the two-fund separation theorem, which states that all investors optimum portfolios will be made up of some combination of an optimal portfolio of risky asset and the risk-free asset. The line representing these possible combinations of risk-free asset and the optimal risky asset portfolio is referred to as the capital allocation line.

Point X on the capital allocation line in Figure 4-5 represents a portfolio that is 40% invested in the risky asset portfolio and 60% invested in the risk-free asset. Its expected return will be $0.40[E(R_{\text{risky asset portfolio}})]+0.60(R_f)$, and its standard deviation will be $0.40(\sigma_{\text{risky asset portfolio}})$.

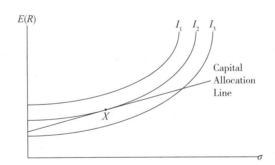

Figure 4-5 Risk-Averse Investor's Indifference Curves

Now that we have constructed a set of the possible efficient portfolios (the capital allocation line),we can combine this with indifference curves representing an individual's preferences for risk and return to illustrate the logic of selecting an optimal portfolio (i.e., one that maximizes the investor's expected utility).In Figure 4-6,we can see that Investor A, with preferences represented by indifference curves I_1, I_2, and I_3, can reach the level of expected utility on I_2 by selecting portfolio X. This is the optimal portfolio for this investor, as any portfolio that lies on I_2 is preferred to all portfolios that lie on I_3 (and in fact to any portfolios that lie between I_2 and I_3).Portfolios on I_1 are preferred to those on I_2,but none of the portfolios that lie on I_1 are available in the market.

The final result of our analysis here is not surprising; investors who are less risk averse will select portfolios that are riskier. Recall that the less an investor's risk aversion, the flatter his indifference curves. As illustrated in Figure 4-6, the flatter indifference curve for Investor B (I_B) results in an optimal (tangency) portfolio that lies to the right of the one that results from a steeper indifference curve, such as that for Investor A (I_A). An investor who is less risk averse should optimally choose a portfolio with more invested in the risky asset portfolio and less invested in the risk-free asset.

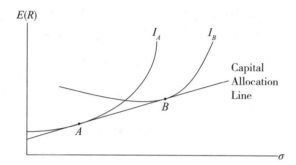

Figure 4-6 Portfolio Choices Based on Investor's Indifference Curves

4.3.5 Systematic Risk and Unsystematic Risk

When an investor diversifies across assets that are not perfectly correlated, the portfolio's risk is less than the weighted average of the risks of individual securities in the portfolio. The risk that is eliminated by diversification is called unsystematic risk. Because the market portfolio contains all risky assets, it must be a well-diversified portfolio. The risk that remains and cannot be diversified is called systematic risk.

The concept of systematic risk applies to individual securities as well as to portfolios. Some securities' returns are highly correlated with overall market returns. Other firms have very little systematic risk.

Total risk can be broken down into its component parts: unsystematic risk and systematic risk. Mathematically:

$$Total\ risk = Unsystematic\ risk + Systematic\ risk$$

Do you actually have to buy all the securities in the market to diversify unsystematic risk? No. Academic studies have shown that as you increase the number of stocks in a portfolio, the portfolio's risk falls toward the level of market risk. One study shows that it only takes about 12 to 18 stocks in a portfolio to achieve 90% of the maximum diversification possible. Another study indicates that it takes 30 securities. Whatever the number, it is significantly less than all the securities.

Figure 4-7 provides a general representation of this concept. Note, in the figure, that once you get to 30 or more securities in a portfolio, the standard deviation remains constant. The remaining risk is systematic, or non-diversifiable risk.

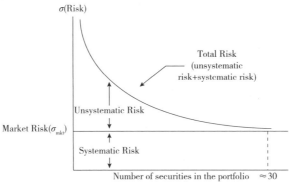

Figure 4-7 Risk vs. Number of Portfolio Assets

4.4 Capital Asset Pricing Model (CAPM)

We know that investors demand a premium for bearing risk; that is, the higher the risk of a security, the higher its expected return must be to induce investors to buy (or to hold) it. However, if investors are primarily concerned with the risk of their portfolio rather than the risk of the individual securities in the portfolio, how should the risk of an individual stock be measured? One answer is provided by the capital asset pricing model (CAPM), an important tool used to analyze the relationship between risk and rates of return. The primary conclusion of the CAPM is this: the relevant risk of an individual stock is its contribution to the risk of a well-diversified portfolio. The stock might be quite risky if held by itself, but if half of its risk can be eliminated by diversification, the relevant risk, which is its contribution to the portfolio's risk, is much smaller than its stand-alone risk.

In finance, the capital asset pricing model (CAPM) is a model used to determine a theoretically appropriate required rate of return of an asset, to make decisions about adding assets to a well-diversified portfolio.

The model takes into account the asset's sensitivity to non-diversifiable risk, often represented by the quantity β in the financial industry, as well as the expected return of the market and the expected return of a theoretical risk-free asset. CAPM assumes a particular form of utility functions (in which only first and second moments matter, that is risk is measured by variance, for example a quadratic utility) or alternatively asset returns whose probability distributions are completely described by the first two moments (for example, the normal distribution) and zero transaction costs (necessary for diversification to get rid of all idiosyncratic risk). Under these conditions, CAPM shows that the cost of equity capital is determined only by beta. Despite it failing numerous empirical tests, and the existence of more modern approaches to asset pricing and portfolio selection, the CAPM still remains popular due to its simplicity and utility in a variety of situations.

The CAPM is a model for pricing an individual security or portfolio. When the expected rate of return for any security is deflated by its beta coefficient, the reward-to-risk ratio for any individual security in the market is equal to the market reward-to-risk ratio, thus

$$\frac{E(R_i)-R_f}{\beta_i}=E(R_m)-R_f$$

The market reward-to-risk ratio is effectively the market risk premium and by rearranging the above equation and solving for $E(R_i)$, we obtain the capital asset pricing model.

$$E(R_i)=R_f+\beta_i\left[E(R_m)-R_f\right]$$

where: $E(R_i)$ = the expected return on the capital asset;

R_f = the risk-free rate of interest such as interest arising from government bonds;

β_i = the sensitivity of the expected excess asset returns to the expected excess market returns;

$E(R_m)$ = the expected return of the market.

Assumptions of CAPM

All investors:

(1) aim to maximize economic utilities (asset quantities are given and fixed).

(2) are rational and risk-averse.

(3) are broadly diversified across a range of investments.

(4) are price takers, i.e., they cannot influence prices.

(5) can lend and borrow unlimited amounts under the risk free rate of interest.

(6) trade without transaction or taxation costs.

(7) deal with securities that are all highly divisible into small parcels (all assets are perfectly divisible and liquid).

(8) have homogeneous expectations.

(9) assume all information is available at the same time to all investors.

Core Words

variance	方差
covariance	协方差
correlation coefficient	相关系数
capital asset pricing model(CAPM)	资本资产定价模型
risk neutrality	风险中性
risk preference	风险偏好
risk premium	风险溢价
risk aversion	风险规避

Key Concepts

1. We can calculate the population variance, σ^2 when we know the return R for each period, the total number of periods (T), and the mean or expected value of the population's distribution (μ), as follows:

$$\sigma^2 = \frac{\sum_{t=1}^{T}(R_t - \mu)^2}{T}$$

2. The portfolio standard deviation can be calculated as follows:

$$\text{Var}(R_p) = \sum_{i=1}^{n} w_i^2 \text{Var}(R_i) + \sum_{i=1}^{n}\sum_{i=1}^{n} w_i w_j \text{COV}(R_i R_j) \qquad (i \neq j)$$

3. Investors can reduce their exposure to individual asset risk by holding a diversifiable portfolio of assets. Diversification may allow for the same portfolio expected return with reduced risk.

4. We obtain the capital asset pricing model (CAPM) as follows:

$$E(R_i) = R_f + \beta_i \left[E(R_m) - R_f \right]$$

Extended Reading

马科维兹投资组合理论

马科维兹(Markowitz)的投资组合理论主要体现在他于1952年发表的论文《证券组合选择》及1959年出版的同名著作中。在投资组合理论中，马科维兹首次将数学中刻画随机变量数字特征的期望和方差引入投资管理的分析框架，对衡量投资风险的基本概念重新进行定义，为投资管理的定量分析提供了理论前提，而且其精巧的数学模型为投资者提供了有效分散投资风险的实际指引。

马科维兹理论的基本前提和假设是：①投资者都是风险规避者，同时收益是不知足的；②假设资产回报率的均值和方差可以比较全面地反映该资产的回报和风险状况，投资者都遵循均值－方差原则；③投资者只进行单期投资决策；④无风险资产是存在的，投资者可以按无风险利率水平借贷；⑤完全信息与齐性预期，也就是说，市场中的投资者不仅对无风险资产的收益率，而且对风险资产收益率的预期及其相关系数都能达成共识；⑥投资风险收益服从正态分布，投资者效用函数是凹的二次函数。

在以上前提和假设下，投资者选择资产时能够追求风险给定下的收益最大化或利润给定下的风险最小化。

资本资产定价模型(CAPM模型)

资本资产定价模型是由美国学者夏普(William Sharpe)等于1964年在资产组合理论的基础上发展起来的，是现代金融市场价格理论的支柱，广泛应用在投资决策和公司理财领域。

资本资产定价模型是在马科维兹理论的基础上推导而来的，为了使模型尽可能地达到研究效果，经济学家们构造了一个相对简化的世界，在这个世界上有相对苛刻的假设条件：①所有投资者都是理性的，意味着投资者追求财富效用的最大化；②所有的投资者选择投资组合的标准为马科维兹的均值方差模型，影响投资决策的主要因素是期望收益率和风险两项；③所有的投资者对资产收益的均值和方差估计相同；④所有的证券投资可以无限制地细分，并可完全变现；⑤所有的投资者都能够以无风险利率、无限制地自由借入和贷出资金，市场上不限制买空和卖空；⑥所有的投资者都可以免费并及时获取市场信息，市场是完全有效的。

CAPM将资产收益与市场组合(即资本市场均衡状态下的均值—方差有效组合)收益之间的协方差同市场组合收益方差之间的比界定为该资产所携带的系统风险。方程表达式为：

$$E(R_i) = R_f + \beta_i \left[E(R_m) - R_f \right]$$

其中：$E(R_i)$是资产i的期望收益率；R_f是无风险利率；$E(R_m)$为市场组合的期望收益率，它是指所有风险资产组成的投资组合；β表示系统风险，是资产i与市场组合收益之间的协方差。

现代资产组合理论的评析

一、马科维兹均值方差理论的缺陷

在理论方面，马科维兹认为"大多数有理性的投资者都是风险厌恶者"这一论点，其真实性值得怀疑。例如，投资者在遇到一种证券能得到7%～23%的收益和另一种证券能得到9%～21%的收益时，他愿意接受前者而放弃后者显然是不理智的，因为两种证券的平均收益都是15%。按马科维兹的理论设想，预期收益和风险的估计是一个组合及其所包括证券的实际收益和风险的正确度量；方差是度量风险的一个最适当的指标等，这些观点难以让人信服。

在实际应用上，马科维兹的理论也存在很大的局限性。首先，实际上许多投资管理人员并不理解其理论中所包含的数学概念，并且认为投资及其管理只是一门艺术而不是科学。其次，利用复杂的数学方法由计算机操作来建立证券组合，需要输入若干统计资料。然而，问题的关键正在于输入资料的正确性。由于大多数收益的预期率是主观的，存在不小的误差，把它作为建立证券组合的输入数据，这就可能使组合还未产生便隐藏着较大幅度的偏误。再次，大量不能预见的意外事件的发生也是潜在的困难。例如，某公司股票的每股盈利若干年来一直在增长，但可能因为股票市场价格的暴跌，其股价立刻随之大幅度下降，从而导致以前对该公司的预计完全失去真实性。此外，证券市场变化频繁，每次变化，都必须对现有组合中的全部证券重新进行评估调整，以保持所需要的风险—收益均衡关系，因此要求连续不断地进行大量数学计算予以保证，这在实践中不但操作难度很大，而且还会造成巨额浪费。

二、资本资产定价模型的局限性

按照资本资产定价模型的构思，应用分析法的投资者愿意接受与市场相等或接近的收益率，排除了投资者获取高于市场收益率的可能性。这种方法否定了证券的选择性和分析家识别优良证券的投资能力。事实证明，建立在大量调研基础上的选择性投资能够取得优异的收益成果。同时，市场指数不一定真正反映全部股票的市场情况，一个投资者完全有可能将其资产组合做得和市场指数一样，但在实际市场上的投资却未必能取得预期的收益。资本资产定价模型假定股票市场是均衡的，而且所有投资者对于股票的预期都是相同的。事实并非如此，在证券投资中，有所谓"最乐观的投资者"和"最悲观的出卖者"，这类现象用资本资产定价模型很难解释。

Questions and Problems

Choose the best answer to the following questions.

1. A measure of how the returns of two risky assets move in relation to each other is the ( ).

   A. range.

   B. covariance.

   C. standard deviation.

   D. expected return.

2. Which of the following statements about risk-averse investors is the most accurate? A risk-averse investor( ).

   A. seeks out the investment with minimum risk, while return is not a major consideration.

   B. will take additional investment risk if sufficiently compensated for the risk.

   C. avoids participating in global equity markets.

   D. seeks out the investment with maximized return, while risk is not a major consideration.

3. A stock with a coefficient of variance of 0.5 has a(an)( ).

   A. variance equal to half the stock's expected return.

   B. expected return equal to half the stock's variance.

   C. expected return equal to half the stock's standard deviation.

   D. standard deviation equal to half the stock's expected return.

4. The covariance of the market's return with a stock's return is 0.005 and the standard deviation of the market's return is 0.05. What is the stock's beta? ( )

   A. 0.5   B. 1.0   C. 1.5   D. 2.0

5. According to the CAPM, what is the expected rate of return of a stock with a beta of 1.2, when the risk-free rate is 6% and the market rate of return is 12%? ( )

   A. 12.8%   B. 12%   C. 8.2%   D. 13.2%

Short answer questions.

1. Define return. Describe the basic calculation involved in finding the return on an investment.

Risk and Return — Chapter 4

2. What is the equation for the capital asset pricing model (CAPM)? Explain the meaning of each variable.

3. Covariance and correlation indicate the extent to which returns move up or down together. Explain the underlying similarities and differences.

4. In the portfolio theory, what is the difference between an efficient portfolio and the optimal portfolio? Is the optimal portfolio for an individual investor always on the efficient frontier? Please state your reasons.

Numerical problems.

1. Consider a game in which a coin will be flipped three times. For each head you will be paid $100. Assume that the coin has a two-thirds probability of coming up heads.

   a. Construct a table of the possibilities and probabilities in this game.

   b. Compute the expected value of the game.

   c. How much would you be willing to pay to play this game?

   d. Consider the effect of a change in the game so that if tails comes up twice in a row, you get nothing. How would your answer to the first three parts of this question change?

2. Assume that the economy can experience high growth, normal growth, or recession. You expect the following stock-market returns for coming year under these conditions.

State of the Economy	Probability	Return
High growth	0.3	30%
Normal growth	0.6	12%
Recession	0.1	−15%

   a. Compute the expected return value of a $1000 investment both in dollars and as a percentage over the coming year.

   b. Compute the standard deviation of the return as a percentage over the coming year.

   c. If the risk-free return is 6%, what is the risk premium for stock-market investment?

3. Consider a portfolio composed of three stocks:

	Weight	E(R)	SD
A	0.3	16%	45%
B	0.3	12%	30%
C	0.4	7%	20%

The covariance between stock A and B is 1.21, between A and C is −0.5, B and C is 0.4. Calculate the portfolio expected return and standard deviation.

4. You can save $ 5,000 per year from your salary and currently have $ 15000 in savings. One year from now you hope to purchase a house for $100,000. To obtain a mortgage you can afford, you will need a down payment equal to 20% of the purchase price of the house. You have two possible investments available. The first is a risk-free bond that pays 5%; the second is the stock-market investment described in **problem 2**. How would you decide which investment to make?

Chapter 5

Categories of Capital Budgeting Projects

Introduction

Capital budgeting is an extremely important aspect of a firm's financial management. Although a single asset usually accounts for a small percentage of a firm's total assets, all capital assets are long-term. Therefore, a firm that makes a mistake in its capital budgeting process has to live with that mistake for a long period of time.

Today's capital expenditure decisions are even more critical than ever. Rapid technological advances, shorter product life cycles, and sophisticated competition make investment decisions vital to the success of a firm.

In this chapter, we show the guidelines for estimating project cash flows and various capital budgeting rules to evaluate and select different projects and deal with conflicts among the methods.

5.1 Capital Budgeting

Capital budgeting process is the process of identifying and evaluating capital projects, that is, projects where the cash flow to the firm will be received over a period longer than a year.

Importance of Capital Budgeting

Any corporate decision with an impact on future earnings can be examined using this framework. Decisions about whether to buy a new machine, expand business in another geographic area, move the corporate headquarters to Beijing, or replace a delivery truck, to name a few, can be examined using a capital budgeting analysis.

For a number of good reasons, capital budgeting may be the most important responsibility that a financial manager has. Firstly, because a capital budgeting decision often involves the purchase of costly long-term assets with lives of many years, the decisions made may determine the future success of the firm. Secondly, the principles underlying the capital budgeting process also apply to other corporate decisions, such as working capital management and making strategic mergers and acquisitions. Finally, making good capital budgeting decisions is consistent with management's primary goal of maximizing shareholder value.

5.2 Project Appraisal

5.2.1 Categories of Capital Budgeting Projects

A replacement project is a capital investment designed to improve efficiency or to maintain or increase revenues by replacing deteriorated or obsolete fixed assets. Replacing outdated equipment or facilities often benefits the firm by lowering its operating costs and preserving its efficiency.

An expansion project is a capital investment designed primarily to enhance revenues by increasing operating capacity in existing products or markets or by focusing operations to expand into completely new products or markets.

Independent projects are projects that are unrelated to each other and allow for each project to be evaluated based on its own profitability. For example, if project A and B are independent, and both projects are profitable, then the firm can accept both projects.

Mutually exclusive project means that only one project in a set of possible projects can be accepted and that the projects compete with each other. If project A and B were mutually exclusive, the firm could accept either project A or project B, but not both.

5.2.2 Are Profit Calculations Useful for Estimating Project Viability?

Accountants often produce a wealth of numerical information about an organization and its individual operations. It is tempting to simply take the profit figures for a project and put these into the (net present value) formula as a substitute for cash flow. A further reason advanced for favoring profit-based evaluations is that managers are often familiar with the notion of "the bottom line" and frequently their performance is judged using profit. However, determining whether a project is "profitable" is not the same as achieving shareholder wealth maximization.

Profit is a concept developed by accountants in order to assist them with auditing and reporting. Profit figures are derived by taking what is a continuous process, a change in a company's worth over time, and allocating these changes to discrete periods of time. This is a difficult task. It is a complex task with rules, principles and conventions in abundance.

Profits often use two carefully defined concepts: income and expenses. Income is not cash inflow, it is the amount earned from business activity whether or not the cash has actually been handed over. So, if a $1,000 sofa has been sold on two years' credit, the accountant's income arises in the year of sale despite the fact that cash actually flows in two years later.

Expense relates to the use of an asset in a particular time period whether or not any cash outflow relating to that item occurs in that period. If a firm pays immediately for a machine that will have a ten-year useful life it does not write off the full cost of the machine against the first year's profit, but allocates a proportion of the cost to each of the next ten years. The cash outflow occurs in the first year, but the expense of the asset occurs over ten years.

Shareholders make current consumption sacrifices, or they give up the return available elsewhere when they choose to invest their money in a firm. They do this in anticipation of receiving more dollars in the future than they laid out. Hence, what is of interest to them are the future cash flows and the precise timing of these cash flows. The accountant does a difficult and important job but the profit figures produced are not suitable for project appraisal. Profit is a poor approach for two main reasons: depreciation and working capital.

5.2.3 Guidelines for Estimating Project Cash Flows

Corporate managers should use cash flows, not accounting profit, because these flows directly affect the firm's ability to pay bills and buy assets.

The capital budgeting process should involve five key principles.

1. Decisions are Based on Cash Flows, not Accounting Income

The relevant cash flows to consider as part of the capital budgeting process are incremental cash flows, the changes in cash flows that will occur if the project is undertaken.

Sunk costs are costs that can not be avoided, even if the project is not undertaken. Because these costs are not affected by the accept/reject decision, they should not be included in the analysis. An example of sunk cost is the consulting fee paid to a marketing research firm to estimate demand for a new product prior to a decision on the project.

Externalities are the effects the acceptance of a project may have on another firm's cash flows. The primary one is a negative externality called cannibalization, which occurs when a new project takes sales from an existing producer. When considering externalities, the full implication of the new project (loss in sales of existing products) should be taken into account. An example of cannibalization is when a soft drink company introduces a diet version of an existing beverage. The analyst should subtract the lost sales of the existing beverage from the expected new sales of the diet version when estimating incremental project cash flows. A positive externality exists when doing the project would have a positive effect on sales of a firm's other product lines.

A project has a conventional cash flow pattern if the sign on the cash flows changes only once, with one or more cash outflows followed by one or more cash inflows. An unconventional cash flow pattern has more than one sign change. For example, a project might have an initial investment outflow, a series of cash inflows, and a cash outflow for asset retirement costs at the end of the project's life.

2. Cash Flows are Based on Opportunity Costs

Opportunity costs are cash flows that a firm loses by undertaking the project under analysis. These are cash flows generated by an asset that a firm already owns that would be forgone if the project under consideration is undertaken. Opportunity costs should be included in project costs. For example, when building a plant, even if the firm already owns the land, the cost of the land should be charged to the project because it could be sold if not used.

3. The Timing of Cash Flows is Important

Capital budgeting decisions account for time value of money, which means that cash flows received earlier are worth more than cash flows to be received later.

4. Cash Flows are Analyzed on an After-tax Basis

The impact of taxes must be considered when analyzing all capital budgeting projects. Firm value is based on cash flows they get to keep, not those they send to government.

5. Financing Costs are Reflected in the Project's Required Rate of Return

Do not consider financing costs specific to the project when estimating incremental cash flows. The discount rate used in the capital budgeting analysis takes account of the firm's cost of capital. Only projects that are expected to return more than the cost of the capital needed to fund them will increase the value of the firm.

5.3 Project Appraisal Rules

5.3.1 Net Present Value (NPV)

NPV is the sum of present values of all the expected incremental cash flow if a project is undertaken. The discount rate used is the firm's cost of capital, adjusted for the risk level of the project. For a normal project, with an initial cash outflow followed by a series of expected after-tax cash inflows, the NPV is the present value of the expected inflows minus the initial cost of the project.

$$NPV = CF_0 + \frac{CF_1}{(1+K)^1} + \frac{CF_2}{(1+K)^2} + \cdots + \frac{CF_n}{(1+K)^n} = \sum_{t=0}^{n} \frac{CF_t}{(1+K)^t}$$

Where: CF_0 = initial investment outlay;

CF_t = after-tax cash flow at time t;

K = required rate of return for project.

A positive NPV project is expected to increase shareholder wealth, a negative NPV project is expected to decrease shareholder wealth, and a zero NPV project has no expected effect on shareholder wealth.

For independent projects, the NPV decision rule is simply to accept any project with a positive NPV and to reject any project with a negative NPV.

Example 5-1

Using the project cash flows presents in Table 5-1, compute the NPV of each project's cash flows and determine for each project whether it should be accepted or rejected.

Assume that the cost of capital is 10%.

Table 5-1 Expected Net After-Tax Cash Flows

Year(t)	Project A	Project B
0	−$2,000	−$2,000
1	1,000	200
2	800	600
3	600	800
4	200	1200

Answer:

$NPV_A = -2000 + 1000/(1.1)^1 + 800/(1.1)^2 + 600/(1.1)^3 + 200/(1.1)^4 = \$157.64$

$NPV_B = -2000 + 200/(1.1)^1 + 600/(1.1)^2 + 800/(1.1)^3 + 1200/(1.1)^4 = \$98.36$

Both project A and project B have positive NPVs, so both should be accepted.

You may calculate the NPV directly by using the cash flow keys on your calculator.

5.3.2 Internal Rate of Return (IRR)

For a normal project, internal rate of return (IRR) is the discount rate that makes the present value of the expected incremental after-tax cash inflows just equal to the initial cost of the project. More generally, IRR is the discount rate that makes the present values of a project's estimated cash inflows equal to the present value of the project's estimated cash outflows. That is, IRR is the discount rate that makes the following relationship hold:

$$PV (\text{inflows}) = PV (\text{outflows})$$

IRR is also the discount rate for which the NPV of the project is equal to zero:

$$NPV = 0 = CF_0 + \frac{CF_1}{(1+IRR)^1} + \frac{CF_2}{(1+IRR)^2} + \cdots + \frac{CF_n}{(1+IRR)^n} = \sum_{t=0}^{n} \frac{CF_t}{(1+IRR)^t}$$

To calculate the IRR, you may use the trial-and-error method. That is, just keep guessing IRRs until you get the right one, or you may use a financial calculator.

IRR decision rule: Firstly, determine the required rate of return for a given project. This is usually the firm's cost of capital. Note that the required rate of return may be higher or lower than the firm's cost of capital to adjust for differences between project risk and the firm's average project risk. Then,

If IRR > the required rate of return, accept the project.

If IRR < the required rate of return, reject the project.

1. The Relative Advantages and Disadvantages of the NPV and IRR Methods

A key advantage of NPV is that it is a direct measure of the expected increase in the value of a firm. NPV is theoretically the best method. Its main weakness is that it does not include any consideration of the size of the project. For example, an NPV of $ 100 is great for a project costing $100 but not so great for a project costing $ 1 million.

A key advantage of IRR is that it measures profitability as a percentage, showing the return on each dollar invested. The IRR provides information on the margin of safety that the NPV does not. From the IRR, we can tell how much below the IRR (estimated return) the actual project return could fall, in percentage terms, before the project becomes uneconomic (has a negative NPV).

The disadvantages of the IRR method are (1) the possibility of producing rankings of mutually exclusive projects that differ from those from NPV analysis and (2) the possibility than a project has multiple IRRs or no IRR.

2. Conflicting Project Rankings

Consider two projects with an initial investment of $ 1,000 and a required rate of return of 10%(Table 5-2). Project X will generate cash inflows of $500 at the end of each of the next five years. Project Y will generate a single cash flow of $ 4,000 at the end of the fifth year.

Table 5-2 Expected Net After-Tax Cash Flows

Year (t)	Project X	Project Y
0	$-1,000	$-1,000
1	500	0
2	500	0
3	500	0
4	500	0
5	500	4,000
NPV	$ 895	$ 1,884
IRR	41%	32%

Project X has a higher IRR, but project Y has a higher NPV. Which is the better project? If project X is selected, the firm will be worth $895 more because the NPV of the expected cash flows is $895 more than the initial cost of the project. Project Y, however, is expected to increase the value of the firm by $1484. Project Y is the better project. Because NPV measures the expected increase in wealth from undertaking a project, NPV is the only acceptable criterion when ranking projects.

Another reason, besides cash flow timing differences, that NPV and IRR may give conflicting project rankings is the difference in project size. Consider two projects, one with an initial outlay of $100,000, and one with an initial outlay of $1million. The smaller project may have a higher IRR, but the increase in the firm's value (NPV) may be small compared to the increase in the firm's value (NPV) of the lager project, even though its IRR is lower.

It is sometimes said that the NPV method implicitly assumes that project cash flows can be reinvested at the discount rate used to calculate NPV. This is a realistic assumption, because it is reasonable to assume that project cash flows could be used to reduce the firm's capital requirements. Any funds that are used to reduce the firm's capital requirements allow the firm to avoid the cost of capital on those funds. Just by reducing its equity capital and debt, the firm could "earn" its cost of capital on funds used to reduce its capital requirements. If we were to rank projects by their IRRs, we could be implicitly assuming that project cash flows could be reinvested at the project's IRR. This is unrealistic and, strictly speaking, if the firm could earn that rate on invested funds, that rate should be the one used to discount project cash flows.

3. The "Multiple IRR" and "No IRR" Problems

If a project has cash outflows during its life or at the end of its life in addition to its initial cash outflows, the project is said to have an unconventional cash flow pattern. Projects with such cash flows may have more than one IRR (there may be more than one discount rate that will produce an NPV equal to zero).

It is also possible to have a project where there is no discount rate that results in a zero NPV, that is, the project does not have an IRR. A project with no IRR may actually be a profitable project. The lack of IRR results from the project having unconventional cash flows, where mathematically, no IRR exists. NPV does not have this problem and produces theoretically correct decision for projects with unconventional cash flow patterns.

Neither of these problems can arise with the NPV method. If a project has non-normal cash flows, the NPV method will give the appropriate accept/reject decision.

5.3.3 Payback Period and Discounted Payback Period

1. Payback Period

The payback period (PP) for a capital investment is the number of years it takes to recover the initial cost of an investment. There is a payback period and discounted payback period. The payback period is determined from the cumulative net cash flow table as follows:

$$\text{Payback period} = \text{Full years until recovery} + \frac{\text{Unrecovered cost at the beginning of the last year}}{\text{Cash flow during the last year}}$$

Generally speaking, the shorter a project's payback, the better. To decide which project(s) to accept, the firm must firstly establish a benchmark payback period.

Decision rule: payback $\leqslant$ the benchmark payback, accept the project.

payback $>$ the benchmark payback, reject the project.

Example 5-2

Calculate the payback periods for the two projects that have the cash flows presented in Table 5-3. Assume that the company set three years as the decision benchmark. Note the year 0 cash flow represents the net cost of each of the projects.

Table 5-3 Expected Net After-Tax Cash Flows($m)

Points in time (yearly intervals)	0	1	2	3	4
Project A	−20	10	8	6	2
Project B	−20	2	6	8	12

Answer:

Note that the cumulative net cash flow (NCF) is just the running total of the cash flows at the end of each time period. Payback will occur when the cumulative NCF equals zero. To find the payback periods construct a table like Table 5-4.

Table 5-4 Cumulative Net Cash Flows ($m)

Year		0	1	2	3	4
Project A	NCF	−20	10	8	6	2
	Cumulative NCF	−20	−10	−2	4	6
Project B	NCF	−20	2	6	8	12
	Cumulative NCF	−20	−18	−12	−4	8

The payback period is determined from the cumulative net cash flow table as follows:

$$\text{Payback period A} = 2 + \frac{2}{6} = 2.33 \text{ years}$$

$$\text{Payback period B} = 3 + \frac{4}{12} = 3.33 \text{ years}$$

Because the decision benchmark is three years, then project B would be accepted and project A would be rejected.

The main drawback of the payback period is that it ignores the time value of money. The payback period ignores cash flows beyond the payback period. This means terminal or salvage value wouldn't be considered. The benefit is that the payback period is a good measure of a project's liquidity and riskiness.

2. Discounted Payback Period

The discounted payback method discounts the estimated cash flows by the project's cost of capital. The Discounted Payback Period (DPP) is the number of years it takes for a project to return its initial investment in current (present value) dollars.

Example 5-3

Compute the discounted payback period for project A and B described in Table 5-5. Assume that the firm's discount rate is 10% and the maximum discounted payback period is three years.

Table 5-5 Cash Flows for Project A and B ($m)

	Year	0	1	2	3	4
Project A	Net cash flow	−20	10	8	6	2
	Discounted NCF	−20	9.10	6.61	4.51	1.37
	Cumulative DNCF	−20	−10.90	−4.29	2.2	1.59
Project B	Net cash flow	−20	2	6	8	12
	Discounted NCF	−20	1.82	4.96	6.01	8.20
	Cumulative DNCF	−20	−18.18	−13.22	−7.21	9.9

Answer:

$$\text{Discounted payback A}: 2 + \frac{4.29}{4.51} = 2.95 \text{ years}$$

$$\text{Discounted payback B}: 3 + \frac{7.21}{8.20} = 3.88 \text{ years}$$

Because the decision benchmark is three years, then project B would be accepted and project A would be rejected.

The drawback of the discounted payback is that it does not consider any cash flows beyond the payback period.

Both the payback and discounted payback give us an indication of a project's risk and liquidity (i.e., the shorter the payback, the greater the liquidity). Payback is a measure of project risk, since distant cash flows are riskier than short term cash flows.

5.3.4 Accounting Rate of Return

The accounting rate of return (ARR) method may be known to readers by other names such as the return on capital employed (ROCE) or return on investment (ROI). The ARR is a ratio of the accounting profit to the investment in the project, expressed as a percentage. The asset's expected accounting rate of return (ARR) is computed by dividing the expected incremental net operating income by the initial investment and then compared to the management's desired rate of return to accept or reject a proposal. If the asset's expected accounting rate of return is greater than or equal to the management's desired rate of return, the proposal is accepted. Otherwise, it is rejected. The accounting rate of return is computed using the following formula:

$$ARR = \frac{Incremental\ accounting\ income}{Initial\ investment} \times 100\%$$

In the above formula, the incremental net operating income is equal to incremental revenues to be generated by the asset less incremental operating expenses. The incremental operating expenses also include depreciation of the asset.

The denominator in the formula is the amount of investment initially required to purchase the asset. If an old asset is replaced with a new one, the amount of initial investment would be reduced by any proceeds realized from the sale of old equipment.

Example 5-4

The TTK Home Appliances Factory wants to replace an old machine with a new one. The old machine can be sold to a small factory for $10,000. The new machine would increase annual revenue by $150,000 and annual operating expenses by $60,000. The new machine would cost $360,000. The estimated useful life of the machine is 12 years with zero salvage value.

Required: compute the accounting rate of return (ARR) of the machine using the above information. Should TTK Home Appliances Factory purchase the machine if management wants an accounting rate of return of 15% on all capital investments?

Answer:

Incremental net operating income

= Incremental revenues − Incremental expenses including depreciation

= 150,000 − (60,000 cash operating expenses + 30,000 depreciation)

= $60,000

The amount of initial investment has been reduced by net realizable value of the old machine (360,000 − 10,000 = $350,000).

$$ARR = 60,000 / 350,000 = 17.14\%$$

According to accounting rate of return method, the TTK Home Appliances Factory should purchase the machine because its estimated accounting rate of return is 17.14%, which is greater than the management's desired rate of return of 15%.

1. Comparison of Different Alternatives

If several investments are proposed and the management has to choose the best due to limited funds, the proposal with the highest accounting rate of return is preferred. Consider the following example:

Example 5-5

The TTK Home Appliances Factory has the following different alternative investment proposals (See Table 5-6):

Table 5-6 Different Alternative Investment Proposals

Items	Proposal A	Proposal B	Proposal C
Expected annual incremental income ($)	50,000	75,000	90,000
Initial investment ($)	250,000	300,000	500,000
Expected accounting rate of return (%)	20	25	18

Required: using accounting rate of return method, select the best investment proposal for the company.

Answer:

If only accounting rate of return is considered, the proposal B is the best proposal for TTK Home Appliances Factory company because its expected accounting rate of return is the highest among three proposals (See Table 5-6).

2. Advantages and Disadvantages of ARR

(1) Advantages

a. Accounting rate of return is simple and straightforward to compute.

b. It focuses on accounting net operating income. Creditors and investors use accounting net operating income to evaluate the performance of management.

(2) Disadvantages

a. Accounting rate of return method does not take into account the time value of money. Under this method a dollar in hand and a dollar to be received in future are considered of equal value.

b. Cash is very important for every business. If an investment quickly generates cash inflow, the company can invest in other profitable projects. But accounting rate of return method focuses on accounting net operating income rather than cash flow.

c. The accounting rate of return does not remain constant over useful life for many projects. A project may, therefore, look desirable in one period but undesirable in another period.

5.4 The Investment Process

There is a great deal more to a successful investment programme than simply project appraisal. As Figure 5-1 demonstrates, project appraisal is one of a number of states in the investment process. The emphasis in the academic world on even more sophistication in appraisal could be seriously misplaced. Attention paid to the evolution of investment ideas, their development and sifting may produce more practical returns. Marrying the evaluation of projects once screened with strategic, resource and human considerations may lead to the avoidance of damaging decisions. Following through the implementation with a review of what went right, what went wrong, and why, may enable better decision making in the future.

Investment by a firm is a process often involving large numbers of individuals up and down an organizational hierarchy. It is a complex and infinitely adaptable process, which is likely to differ from one organization to another. However, we can identify some common threads.

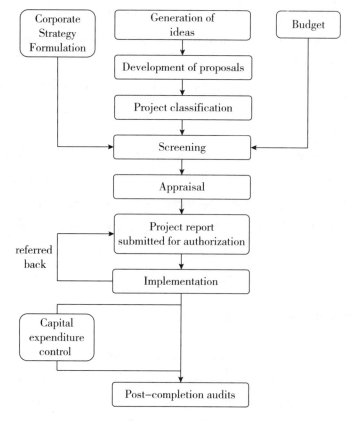

Figure 5-1 The investment process

Core Words

capital budgeting	资本预算
payback period	投资回收期
discounted payback period	动态投资回收期
accounting rate of return	会计收益率
operating income	营业收入
return on investment (ROI)	投资报酬率
initial investment	期初投资
cumulative net cash flow	累积净现金流
discounted cash flow	折现现金流
independent project	独立项目

replacement project	更新项目
incremental cash flow	增量现金流
opportunity cost	机会成本
sunk cost	沉没成本
expansion project	扩充项目
net present value	净现值
internal rate of return	内部收益率
mutually exclusive project	互斥项目

Key Concepts

1. Capital budgeting process is the process of identifying and evaluating capital projects, that is, projects where the cash flow to the firm will be received over a period longer than a year.

2. Categories of capital budgeting projects include: replacement projects, expansion projects, independent projects and mutually exclusive projects.

3. NPV is the sum of present values of all the expected incremental cash flow if a project is undertaken. The discount rate used is the firm's cost of capital, adjusted for the risk level of the project.

4. IRR is the discount rate that makes the present value of a project's estimated cash inflows equal to the present value of the project's estimated cash outflows.

5. A key advantage of NPV is that it is a direct measure of the expected increase in the value of a firm. NPV is theoretically the best method. A key advantage of IRR is that it measures profitability as a percentage, showing the return of each dollar invested. The disadvantages of the IRR method are ①the possibility of producing rankings of mutually exclusive projects that differs from those from NPV analysis and ② the possibility that a project has multiple IRRs or no IRR.

6. Payback period is the number of years required to recover the original cost of the investment.

7. Discounted payback period method discounts the estimated cash flows by the project's cost of capital, then calculates the time it takes to recover the investment.

8. Accounting rate of return is a financial ratio used in capital budgeting. ARR calculates the return, generated from net income of the proposed capital investment. The ARR is a percentage return.

Extended Reading

项目的类型和评价过程

项目是指有明确目标的一系列复杂且相互关联的活动。公司尤其是实业公司为实现增长，进而达到财务管理目标，往往要进行项目投资。开发新产品、建造生产线都是实业公司的重要项目，需要投入资本等资源并需要进行项目的资本预算。开发新产品、建造生产线项目，具有目标性、长期性、唯一性、不可逆性等基本特征。

一、项目的类型

经营性长期资产投资项目可分为五种类型。

(1) 新产品开发或现有产品的规模扩张项目。通常需要添置新的固定资产，并增加企业的营业现金流量。

(2) 设备或厂房的更新项目。通常需要更换固定资产，但不改变企业的经营现金收入。

(3) 研究与开发项目。通常不直接产生现实的收益，而是得到一项是否投产新产品的选择权。

(4) 勘探项目。通常使企业得到一些有价值的信息。

(5) 其他项目，包括劳动保护设施建设、购置污染控制装置等。这些决策不直接产生营业现金流入，但能使企业在履行社会责任方面的形象得到改善。它们有可能减少未来的现金流入。

这些投资项目的现金流量分布有不同的特征，具体的分析方法也有区别。最具一般意义的是第一种投资，即添置新的固定资产。

二、项目评价的程序

投资项目的评价一般包含下列几个步骤。

(1) 提出各种项目的投资方案。新产品方案通常来自研发部门或营销部门，设备更新的建议通常来自生产部门等。

(2) 估计投资方案的相关现金流量。

(3) 计算投资方案的价值指标,如净现值、内部收益率等。
(4) 比较价值指标与可接受标准。
(5) 对已接受的方案进行再评价。

互斥项目的优选问题

互斥项目,是指接受一个项目就必须放弃另一个项目的情况。通常,它们是为解决一个问题而设计的两个备选方案。例如,为了生产一个新产品,可以选择进口设备,也可以选择国产设备,它们的使用寿命、购置价格和生产能力均不同。企业只需购买其中之一就可解决目前的问题,而不会同时购置。

针对互斥项目,仅仅评价哪一个项目方案可以接受是不够的,如果两者都有正的净现值,我们需要知道哪一个更好。如果一个项目方案的所有评价指标,包括净现值、内部收益率、投资回收期和会计收益率,均比另一个项目方案好,我们在选择时不会有什么困扰。问题是这些评价指标出现矛盾时,尤其是评价的基本指标——净现值和内部收益率出现矛盾时,我们该如何选择?

评价指标出现矛盾的原因主要有两种:一是投资额不同,二是项目寿命不同。如果是投资额不同引起的(项目的寿命相同),对于互斥项目应当以净现值法优先,因为它可以给股东带来更多的财富。股东需要的是实实在在的报酬,而不是报酬的比率。

如果净现值与内部收益率的矛盾是项目有效期不同引起的,我们有两种解决方法:一个是共同年限法,另一个是等额年金法。

一、共同年限法

如果两个互斥项目不仅投资额不同,而且项目期限不同,则其净现值没有可比性。例如,一个项目投资3年创造了较少的净现值,另一个项目投资6年创造了较多的净现值,后者的盈利性不一定比前者好。

共同年限法的原理是:假设投资项目可以在终止时进行重置,通过重置使两个项目达到相同的年限,然后比较其净现值。该方法也被称为重置价值链法。

二、等额年金法

等额年金法是用于不同年限互斥项目比较的另一种方法。它比共同年限法要简单。其计算步骤如下。

(1) 计算两个项目的净现值。
(2) 计算净现值的等额年金额,公式如下:

$$等额年金额 = 净现值 / 年金现值系数$$

(3) 假设项目可以无限重置,并且每次都在该项目的终止期,等额年金的资本化就是项目的净现值。

以上两种分析方法有区别。共同年限法比较直观，易于理解，但是预计现金流的工作很困难。等额年金法应用简单，但不便于理解。

两种方法存在共同的缺点：①有的领域技术进步快，目前就可以预期升级换代不可避免，不可能原样复制；②如果通货膨胀比较严重，必须考虑重置成本的上升，这是一个非常具有挑战性的任务，两种方法对此都没有考虑；③从长期来看，竞争会使项目净利润下降，甚至被淘汰，两种方法在分析时都没有对此进行考虑。

通常在实务中，只有重置概率很高的项目才适宜采用上述分析方法。对于预计项目年限差别不大的项目，直接比较净现值，不需要做重置现金流的分析，因为预计现金流量和资本成本的误差比年限差别还大。

资本预算管理

资本预算管理首先是置于公司治理背景下的一种全方位的行为管理，它涉及预算权限的划分与预算责任的落实；其次，它是一种全员参与式的管理，也就是说，预算不等于财务计划，预算管理不等于财务部门管理；最后，预算管理是一种机制，它能做到责任、权利与义务的对等，将预算约束与预算激励对等地运用到各预算主体之中。同样的道理，如果将资本预算管理纳入预算管理的范围，不难发现，资本预算管理不再也不可能单纯地表现为财务预算方法，它是将预算方法融入预算管理之中，从价值管理与行为管理两方面对资本支出在不同项目间进行分配、规划与控制的一种管理行为。它至少包括：①从价值管理角度看，它主要解决项目可行性及其选择问题，这也是西方资本预算理论的核心内容；②从行为管理角度看，它主要解决资本预算主体的定位及其相应的责权利对等关系。总之，资本预算管理不等于资本预算，资本预算管理应当成为控制项目资本超支现象最有效的手段。

Questions and Problems

Choose the best answer to the following questions.

1. Which of the following statements about the payback period method is false? (   )

   A. Payback period provides a rough measure of a project's liquidity and risk.

   B. Payback method considers all cash flows throughout the entire life of a project.

   C. Cumulative net cash flow is the running total through time of a project's cash flow.

   D. Payback period is the number of years it takes to recover the original cost of the investment.

2. Which of the following statements is false? The discounted payback: (   )

A. method frequently ignores terminal values.

B. method can give conflicting results with the NPV.

C. period is generally shorter than the regular payback.

D. period is the time it takes for the present value of the project cash inflows to equal the cost of the investment.

3. Which is the following statements about NPV and IRR is least accurate? (   )

A. The IRR is the discount rate that equates the present value of the cash inflows with the present value of outflows.

B. For mutually exclusive projects, if the NPV method and the IRR method give conflicting rankings, the analyst should use the IRRs to select the project.

C. The NPV method assumes that cash flows will be reinvested at the cost of capital, while IRR ranking implicitly assumes that cash flows are reinvested at the IRR.

D. The IRR is the discount rate that equates the present value of the cash inflows.

4. Which of the following statements about NPV and IRR is least accurate? (   )

A. The IRR can be positive even if the IRR is negative.

B. When the IRR equals the cost of capital, the NPV will be 0.

C. The NPV will be positive if the IRR is less than the cost of capital.

D. The NPV will be negative if the IRR is less than the cost of capital.

Use the following data to answer question 5 ~ 8.

ATC Company is considering the purchase of equipment that costs $5,000. Assume a cost of capital of 10 percent and the following cash flow schedule:

Year 1: $3,000   Year 2: $2,000   Year 3: $2,000

5. What is the project's payback period? (   )

A. 1.5 years   B. 2.0 years   C. 2.5 years   D. 3.0 years

6. What is the project's discounted payback period? (   )

A. 1.4 years   B. 2.0 years   C. 2.4 years   D. 2.6 years

7. What is the project's NPV? (   )

A. −$309   B. +$243   C. +$883   D. +$1,523

8. What is the project's IRR (approximately)? (   )

A. 5%   B. 10%   C. 15%   D. 21%

Chapter 6
Cost of Capital

Cost of Capital — Chapter 6

Introduction

Trillions of dollars are disclosed on the statement of financial position to show the financial situation on a specific date of a company. As we know, Companies raise money in different ways from the capital market. They have to pay a price to obtain funds as capital providers make their investments expecting to make a return. This is the cost of capital.

Cost of capital is a key point for companies when making financing decisions. What kinds of financing methods chosen and how much for each method are two main questions, which should be considered by financial managers. This chapter will illustrate the definition of cost of capital, individual cost capital for each type of financing and how to compute the cost of capital of a firm.

6.1 Introduction to the Cost of Capital

6.1.1 Source of Finance

A company could not run without capital injection. However, the company itself does not own the funds. They should obtain the capital in the capital market. Most companies raise money using a combination of debt and equity. Debt is composed of two forms, which are short-term debt and long-term debt. And the equity is a long-term concept, which includes preferred stock, common stock and retained earning. This chapter will focus on the long-term capital, which is shown in Figure 6-1.

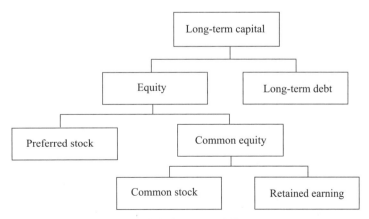

Figure 6-1 Source of finance

6.1.2　What is the Cost of Capital?

Cost of capital is the price that a company should pay for achieving capital from investors, including shareholders and creditors. It is the minimum rate of return that capital providers to earn in the best alternative investment with the same or similar risk and duration. Therefore, the cost of capital is the minimum rate of return or the opportunity cost of a company's investors.

6.1.3　General Model to Estimate the Cost of Capital

Cost of capital could be expressed by both amount and ratio. We always estimate the cost of capital ratio instead of the cost amount in corporate finance. It refers to the discount rate, when a company obtains a net amount of capital from different sources equal to the present value of the expected future cash outflow. Net amount of capital is the remaining part of all the capital that a company receives after deducting all kinds of financing costs, such as flotation cost of securities and service expenses of banks and other financial institutions. Future cash outflow is the dividend, interest and principal paid by a company in a future. Cost of capital should be estimated as:

$$P_0(1-f) = \frac{CF_1}{(1+K)} + \frac{CF_2}{(1+K)^2} + \cdots \frac{CF_n}{(1+K)^n}$$

Where: K = the cost of capital;

CF_n = the cash flow paid to capital providers (dividend, interest and principal paid) at year n;

P_0 = the total capital amount;

f = the ratio of financing cost.

6.2　Cost of Debt

Debt is one of the main financing types for corporations. Debt results in tax savings because interest payments are deducted from the company's income before corporation income tax is levied. Therefore, debt will reduce the amount of taxable income of a firm. The cost of debt financing is related to:

- The interest payable on the borrowed money.
- The net amount of debt which is involved and the related direct financing costs.
- A firm's tax rate.

Cost of debt can be calculated as follows:

$$P_0(1-f) = \sum_{t=1}^{N} \frac{P_t + I_t(1-T)}{(1+K_d)^t}$$

Where: K_d = the cost of debt;

P_0 = the market value of debt, which is the present value of debt;

f = the ratio of financing cost;

P_t = the principle to repay at t period;

I_t = interest paid at t period;

N = the time to maturity of the debt;

T = the income tax rate.

Example 6-1

THK Inc. gets a $2,000 million 5-year loan from the bank with 5% interest rate per year. The direct cost for the loan is 0.3% of the total amount. The tax rate of THK Inc. is 20%.

Requirement: calculate the cost of debt of THK .

Solution:

$$2000 \times (1 - 0.3\%) = \sum_{t=1}^{5} \frac{2000 \times 5\% \times (1-20\%)}{(1+K_d)^t} + \frac{2000}{(1+K_d)^5}$$

Here, the cost of debt is 4.07% by applying Excel.

6.3 Cost of Equity

6.3.1 Cost of Preferred Stock

Preferred stock is a type of equity with fixed dividends paid to shareholders forever. Its dividends will be paid after tax but before the payment of common stock dividends. However, preference shareholders do not have voting rights except the voting related to them. The cost of preferred stock will be equal to the rate of return that investors are required on this type of stock. Cost of preferred stocks is the ratio of the dividends paid divided by the market price of preferred stocks.

$$\text{Cost of preferred stock } K_p = \frac{D_p}{P_n}$$

Where: D_p = dividend on preferred stocks;

P_n = net preferred price = preferred price − flotation cost.

Example 6-2

THK Inc. has issued preferred stocks that are paying $15 dividend per share and the preferred stocks are currently trading at $100 each.

Requirement: estimate the cost of preferred stocks.

Solution:

$$\text{Cost of preferred stocks } K_p = \frac{15}{100} \times 100\% = 15\%$$

6.3.2 Cost of Common Equity

There are two ways for companies to increase common equity – common stock and retained earnings. Issuing common stocks is the direct way and reinvesting earnings instead of paid dividends outside of company is the indirect way.

1. Cost of Retained Earnings

(1) Retained Earnings

Earnings obtained by a company could either be paid to shareholders as dividends or remain in the company for reinvestment. Retained earnings are the earnings left in a company. If the company chooses to pay earnings to stockholders as dividends, the shareholders can use the funds to invest in other securities and financial instruments. If the company chooses to keep the earnings, it means that the shareholders give up the opportunity to invest in other ways as they can achieve more benefits reinvesting in the company. Therefore, the cost of retained earnings is the opportunity cost. The company must earn at least as much as the shareholders can obtain on another investment with similar risk if leaving the earnings for reinvestment. This means that the cost of retained earnings is based on the required rate of return on the company's common stocks.

(2) Approaches to Estimate the Cost of Retained Earnings

Cost of retained earnings can be calculated by two main methods – capital asset pricing model (CAPM) and discount cash flow model. For this chapter, cash flow focuses on the dividends particularly.

a. Estimate the cost of retained earnings by discount cash flow model

The dividend discount model is a method to compute the value of equity by dividends discount at the discount rate. The discount rate is usually the minimum required return rate of investors. As mentioned above, the cost of capital refers to the same as the minimum required rate of return. To estimate the cost of equity is to compute the discount rate in the dividend discount model. This chapter focuses on constant growth rate shares.

Cost of Capital — Chapter 6

As the value of share is:

$$Value\ per\ share = \sum_{t=1}^{n} \frac{D_t}{(1+r)^t}$$

Where: D = expected dividends per share at t period;

r = required return rate of investors.

The cost of capital is equal to the r in this equation. If the dividends are expected to grow at a constant rate, then the price can be expressed as:

$$Current\ price\ per\ share\ P_0 = \frac{D_1}{r-g} = \frac{D_0(1+g)}{r-g}$$

Where: P_0 = current price per share;

D_1 = expected dividends next period;

D_0 = expected dividends at present period;

r = required return rate of investors;

g = expected stable growth rate in perpetuity and $r > g$.

Therefore, the cost of retained earnings can be referred as

$$Cost\ of\ retained\ earning\ K_e = \frac{D_1}{P_0} + g$$

This implies that investors will expect to receive the dividend yield plus some capital gains.

> *Example 6-3*
>
> THK Inc. has expected dividends of $2.50 next year, the share price is $20 currently and the growth rate is constant at 8%.
>
> **Requirement:** estimate the cost of retained earnings.
>
> **Solution:**
>
> $$Cost\ of\ retained\ earning = \frac{2.5}{20} + 8\% = 20.5\%$$

b. Estimate the cost of retained earnings by CAPM

The capital asset price model, as we learned from the previous chapter, could be applied for examining the cost of retained earnings as the return of capital is based on the risk of capital. CAPM is a model often represented by the quantity beta (β), which shows the relationship between the returns on a firm's shares and stock market movements in financial industry; as well as the expected returns of the market which are returns on all investment assets in the market and the expected return of a theoretical risk-free asset. By using CAPM, the cost of equity is expressed as:

$$\text{Cost of retained earning } K_e = K_f + \beta(K_m - K_f)$$

Where: K_f = the risk free rate;

K_m = the rate of return on the market;

β = the relationship between the returns on a firm's shares and stock market movements.

> ***Example 6-4***
>
> THK Inc. is a firm, which has a beta coefficient of 1.2, the rate of return on the market is 12% and the treasury bill rate, referring the risk free rate is 8%.
>
> **Requirement:** estimate the cost of retained earnings.
>
> **Solution:**
>
> $$\text{Cost of retained earning} = 8\% + 1.2 \times (12\% - 8\%) = 12.8\%$$

2. Cost of Common Stocks

An alternative to achieve common equity is the issue of new shares. Most companies prefer to hire a banker to assist them to issue stocks as this is a complex task. The costs of issuing new shares are often called flotation costs. These costs need to be taken into account when evaluating equity that is funded in this manner.

To estimate the cost of common shares is quite similar to computing the cost of retained earnings. The only factor, which is different, is the flotation cost. If the shares are expected to grow at a constant rate, the cost of common shares is:

$$\text{Cost of common stock } K_S = \frac{D_1}{P_0(1-f)} + g$$

Where: P_0 = current price per share;

D_1 = expected dividends next period;

g = expected stable growth rate in perpetuity;

f = the rate of flotation expense to issue shares.

> ***Example 6-5***
>
> THK Inc. has issued 6,000,000 new shares, and it expects dividends of $1.50 next year. The issue price is $20 and the rate of flotation cost is 5%. It forecasts that the sustainable dividends growth rate is at 8%.
>
> **Requirement:** estimate the cost of common stock.
>
> **Solution:**
>
> $$\text{Cost of common stock} = \frac{1.5}{20 \times (1 - 5\%)} + 8\% = 15.89\%$$

6.4 Weighted Average Cost of Capital

6.4.1 What is the Weighted Average Cost of Capital?

Weighted average cost of capital (WACC) is the weighted average of the component costs of types used by a firm to finance its investments. Most companies always finance their investment using a mix of different ways instead of a signal financing source. The mix is the capital structure, which will be talked about in the following chapter. The target of financing is to minimize the weighted average cost of capital.

Weighted average cost of capital is determined by the individual cost of capital and the portion of each source of financing. Therefore, WACC can be expressed as:

$$\text{Weighted average cost of } r_{WACC} = \sum_{j=1}^{n} K_j W_j$$

Where: K_j = individual cost of capital;

W_j = portion of individual financing source.

Example 6-6

THK Inc. raises its $100,000 funds in the following manners(Table 6-1).

Table 6-1 Financing source of THK

Source	Amount	Cost of capital
Debt	$40,000	7%
Preference shares	$20,000	11%
Common shares	$40,000	14%
Total	$100,000	—

Requirement: calculate the WACC of THK.

Solution:

Portion of debt = 40,000 ÷ 100,000 = 40%

Portion of preference share = 20,000 ÷ 100,000 = 20%

Portion of common share = 40,000 ÷ 100,000 = 40%

WACC = 7% × 40% + 11% × 20% + 14% × 40% = 10.6%

6.4.2 Factors Affecting the Weighted Average Cost of Capital

Many factors will have influences on the weighted average cost of capital. Some elements can be controlled by companies while the others are out of their control.

1. Factors Controlled by Company

Three elements in this section will be illustrated. The first one is the capital structure.

The company could choose the sources of financing and the amount of each source. This will have effects on W_i in the equation of WACC. Additionally, dividend policy is another way to affect WACC as it determines the cost of equity to some extent. The last one to mention is the investment policy. The cost of capital reflects the average risk of existing assets in the company. If the risks of projects in which the company invests are higher than those of existing assets, the average risk of company assets will increase leading the cost of capital to rise.

2. Factors Uncontrolled by Company

Interest rates and tax rates are two elements that a company can not control. As for the interest rate, it will affect the cash flow of interest that companies pay on debt, which will influence the cost of debt. If the interest rate increases, the cost of debt will go up. For the income tax rate, as it appears in the calculation of the cost of debt, the change of tax rates can affect WACC. Meanwhile, the capital gain tax is another factor to impact on the expectation of shares that leads to the change of WACC of a company. If the rate of capital gain tax rises, the share will be less desirable and the company tends to arrive the capital by debts. This will affect the W_j of WACC.

WACC is a popular method for a company to estimate its capital costs that provides information in financing and investment decisions. Only when the expected return rate is higher than the weighted average cost of capital will the company accept the investment.

Core Words

cost of capital	资本成本
preferred stock	优先股
common stock	普通股
retained earning	留存收益
net financing amount	筹资净额
cost of debt	债务成本
cost of equity	权益成本
capital asset price model	资本资产定价模型
flotation expense	发行费用
weighted average cost of capital	加权平均资本成本
capital structure	资本结构
individual cost of capital	个别资本成本

dividend policy	股利政策
capital gain tax	资本利得税

Key Concepts

1. Financing is one of the most significant activities in corporate operating. Companies can raise the money from different sources.

2. In the long-term, firms can obtain funds from debt and equity.

3. Cost of capital is the price that a company should pay for achieving capital from investors, including shareholders and creditors. It is the minimum rate of return or opportunity cost of a company's investors.

4. To estimate the cost of debts, the net amount of borrowing, the related interest rate and the level of tax rate should be taken into account.

5. Preferred stocks, common stocks and retained earnings are three equity-financing methods.

6. Cost of retained earning can be calculated with two approaches: the discount cash flow model and capital assets price model.

7. Weighted average cost of capital (WACC) is the weighted average of the component costs of types used by a firm to finance its investments. The best capital structure can be expressed by the minimum of weighted average cost of capital.

Extended Reading

资本成本的作用

首先，资本成本是筹资决策的重要依据。企业的资金可以通过各种渠道，如银行信贷资金、民间资金、企业资金等获得，其筹资的方式也多种多样，如吸收直接投资、发行股票、银行借款、融资租赁、内部融资等。但不管选择何种渠道，采用哪种方式，主要考虑的因素还是资本成本。

通过不同渠道和方式所筹措的资本，将会形成不同的资本结构，由此产生不同的财务风险和资本成本。所以，资本成本也就成了确定最佳资本结构的主要因素之一。

随着筹资数量的增加，资本成本将随之变化。当筹资数量增加到增资的成本大于增资的收入时，企业便不能再追加资本。因此，资本成本是限制企业筹资数额的一个重要因素。

第二，资本成本是评价和选择投资项目的重要标准。资本成本可以用来表示投资者应当取得的最低报酬水平。只有当投资项目的收益高于资本成本的情况下，才值得为之筹措资本；反之，就应该放弃该投资机会。

第三，资本成本是衡量企业资金效益的临界基准。如果一定时期的综合资本成本率高于总资产报酬率，就说明企业资本的运用效益差，经营业绩不佳；反之，则说明企业资本的运用效益良好，经营业绩佳。

加权平均资本成本的局限性

虽然加权平均资本成本在企业筹资决策中的应用非常广泛，但是其本身也存在一定的局限性。

首先，在计算权重的过程中，究竟采用相关资本的市场价值还是账面价值。从理论上来说，应该采用市场价值进行相应的计算，但在现实中一些债务的市场价值很难获得，因而采用账面价值进行计算。从财务的角度，账面价值在某种程度上并不能完全反映相关资本的真实价值。这样计算出来的加权平均资本成本可能在一定程度上存在偏差。

其次，在加权平均资本成本的相关假设中，我们假设企业的资本结构在一定时期内是保持不变的。但在企业的实际经营当中，企业的资本是流动的。如果企业的资本结构在短期内连续发生较大的变化，就很难应用加权平均资本成本。

最后，按照税法的规定，一些企业具有暂时不需要纳税的优惠，比如由于企业亏损延迟缴纳税款和高新技术企业符合条件的技术转让所得免征、减征企业所得税等。此时如果使用WACC方法，这种由于税收庇护所产生的价值增加就无法清晰明了地揭示出来，不利于对企业价值的评估。

Questions and Problems

Choose the best answer to the following questions.

1. Which of the following items is not a long-term financing resource? (　　)

　A. Common stock.

B. Retained earnings.

C. Account payable.

D. Preferred stock.

2. Cost of capital is (　　).

A. the price a company pays for capital providers.

B. the cost of each financing component multiplied by that component's percent of the total borrowed.

C. IRR.

D. all of the above.

3. Which of the following would be classified as equity financing for a firm? (　　)

A. Preferred shareholders, nonbank lenders and suppliers.

B. Nonbank lenders, retained earnings and commercial banks.

C. Preferred shareholders, common shareholders and retained earnings.

D. banks, nonbank lenders and common shareholders.

4. Which of the following illustrations about cost of capital is not correct? (　　)

A. Cost of capital is the opportunity cost.

B. Cost of capital is the minimum return of investors.

C. Cost of capital can be the discount rate when estimating security values.

D. Cost of capital can be only presented as an amount.

5. Which method of calculating a firm's cost of equity is most likely to incorporate the long-run return relationship between the firm's stock and the market portfolio? (　　)

A. Dividend discount model.

B. Bond-yield-plus risk-premium.

C. Capital asset pricing model.

D. FCFE model.

6. Weighted average cost of capital is (　　).

A. the average of the cost of each financing component, weighted by the proportion of each component.

B. the cost of capital for a firm as a whole.

C. made up of two long-term financing components: the cost of debt and the cost of equity

D. all of the above.

7. Cost of retained earnings is (　　).

A. the loss of the dividend option for the owners.

B. the cost of issuing new common stock without the flotation costs.

C. the cost of capital for the common shareholders.

D. all of the above.

8. Which of the following is tax-deductible expenses for a firm? (   )

A. Interest expenses.

B. Preferred stock dividends.

C. Common stock dividends.

D. Retained earnings.

9. Which of the following illustrations is correct? (   )

A. The best capital structure can be expressed by the minimum of weighted average cost of capital.

B. Retained earnings do not have cost of capital.

C. The cost of equity is usually lowers than the cost of debt.

D. Income may affect the cost of equity.

10. Which of these items cannot affect the weighted average cost of capital? (   )

A. The individual cost of capital.

B. Income tax.

C. Accounting judgment.

D. Proportion of each type of cost of capital.

Numerical problems.

1. EX Inc. gets a $550 million 5-year loan from the bank with 8% interest rate. The direct cost for the loan is 0.1% of the total amount. The tax rate of EX is 25%.

Requirement: calculate the cost of debt of EX.

2. PO company has issued preferred stocks with $24 dividend per share and the preferred stocks are currently trading at $55 each.

Requirement: estimate the cost of preferred stocks.

3. XYZ is a firm, which has a beta coefficient of 1.5, the rate of return on the market is 14% and the treasury bill rate is 7%.

Requirement: estimate the cost of retained earnings.

4. VL company has issued 5,000,000 new shares, and it has expected dividends of $4.50 next year with constant growth rate at 6%. The share price is $15, the rate of flotation cost is 0.4%.

Requirement: estimate the cost of common stock.

5. AL company finances $2,000,000 funds in three ways. $500,000 is raised from debt with an interest rate at 5%; $800,000 is financed by issuing preferred stocks at $15 per share and $700,000 is raised by issuing common stocks at $20 per share. The dividends policy for AL is that it pays $5 per share for preferred stocks and $6 per share for common stocks. The common stock is expected at a growth rate of 4%. The tax rate in AL is 25%.

Requirement: estimate the weighted average cost of capital.

Part III

Financing Decision

Chapter 7
Capital Structure

Capital Structure Chapter 7

Introduction

Someone has to decide what is an appropriate level of borrowing for a firm given its equity capital base. The fundamental question of this chapter is: if future cash flow generated by the business is assumed to be constant, can managers increase shareholder value simply by altering the proportion of debt in the total capital structure? If this is possible then surely managers have a duty to move the firm towards the optimal debt proportion.

Capital structure of a firm refers to the mix of long-term finances used by the firm. In short, it is the financing plan of the firm. With the objective of maximizing the value of the equity shares, choice should be the pattern of using debt and equity in a proportion that will lead towards the achievement of the firm's objective. The capital structure should add value to the firm. Financing mix decisions are investment decisions and have no impact on the operating the earnings of the firm. Such decisions influence the firm's value through the earnings available to the shareholders.

The value of a firm is dependent on its expected future earnings and the required rate of return. The objective of any firm is to have an ideal mix of permanent sources of funds in a manner that will maximize the firm's market price. The proper mix of funds is referred to as the optimal capital structure.

7.1 Leverage Analysis

Leverage analysis is a tool that is usually used by financial managers for financial analysis. In order to facilitate the analysis, we make the following assumptions: ①The company only sells one kind of product and the selling price is constant; ②The unit variable cost and total fixed cost of operating costs remain unchanged within the relevant scope.

7.1.1 Operating Leverage

Operating leverage is the trade-off between variable costs and fixed costs. High operating leverage generally produces a higher expected rate of return. A firm is said to have high operating leverage if a high percentage of its total costs is fixed. Holding all else constant, high operating leverage indicates that a small change in sales will cause a large change in operating income.

The degree of operating leverage (DOL) is defined as the percentage change in earnings before interest and taxes (EBIT) that results from a given percentage change in sales:

$$DOL = \frac{\text{percentage change in EBIT}}{\text{percentage change in sales}} = \frac{\Delta EBIT / EBIT}{\Delta Q / Q}$$

Another way to estimate DOL is:

$$DOL = \frac{Q(P-V)}{Q(P-V)-F} = \frac{Q(P-V)}{EBIT}$$

Where: Q = sales quantity of the product;

P = product unit price;

V = unit variable cost;

F = total fixed cost;

EBIT = earnings before interest and taxes.

If fixed costs are zero, DOL = 1 since there is no operating leverage.

Example 7-1

THH Ltd. produces only one product — A product. The current sales quantity is 20,000 unit, product price is $5/unit, unit variable cost is $3, total fixed cost is $20,000. Assume the unit price and the level of cost will be constant, calculate the degree of operating leverage for the company.

Answer:

$$DOL = \frac{Q(P-V)}{Q(P-V)-F} = \frac{20{,}000(5-3)}{20{,}000(5-3)-20{,}000} = 2$$

7.1.2 Financial Leverage

Financial leverage refers to the use of fixed-income securities, like debt and preferred stock. Financial leverage magnifies the variability of earnings per share due to the existence of the required interest payments.

The degree of financial leverage (DFL) measures the percentage change in earnings per share (EPS) for a given percentage change in earnings before interest and taxes (EBIT):

$$DFL = \frac{\text{percentage change in EPS}}{\text{percentage change in EBIT}} = \frac{\Delta EPS / EPS}{\Delta EBIT / EBIT}$$

Another way to estimate DFL is:

$$DFL = \frac{EBIT}{EBIT - I - D/(1-T)}$$

Where: EPS = earnings per share;

I = interest;

D = preferred shares dividend;

T = income tax rate;

EBIT = earnings before interest and taxes.

If interest is zero (no debt), DFL = 1 since there is no financial leverage.

Example 7-2

Assume that THH Ltd. has $100,000 in sales, variable costs of 70% of sales, fixed costs of $10,000, and an annual interest expense of $1,500. The preferred shares dividend for the year is $3,000 and the income tax rate 25%. If THH's EBIT increases by 10%, by how much will its earnings per share increase?

Answer:

Sales	$100,000
Operating Cost	−$70,000
Fixed cost	−$10,000
EBIT	$20,000

$$DFL = \frac{EBIT}{EBIT - I - D/(1-T)} = \frac{20,000}{20,000 - 1,500 - 3,000/(1-25\%)} \approx 1.38$$

Hence, earnings per share will increase by:

$$\frac{\Delta EPS}{EPS} = \frac{\Delta EBIT}{EBIT} \times DFL = 10\% \times 1.38 = 13.8\%$$

7.1.3 Total Leverage

If a firm is exposed to a high degree of both operating leverage and financial leverage, slight changes in sales will lead to large fluctuations in EPS, i. e. total leverage.

Degree of total leverage (DTL) combines the degree of operating leverage and financial leverage. DTL measures the extent to which a given change in sales will affect EPS. DTL is computed as:

$$DTL = DOL \times DFL = \frac{\Delta EBIT/EBIT}{\Delta Q/Q} \times \frac{\Delta EPS/EPS}{\Delta EBIT/EBIT} = \frac{\Delta EPS/EPS}{\Delta Q/Q}$$

Another way to estimate DTL is:

$$DTL = \frac{Q(P-V)}{EBIT - I - D/(1-T)}$$

Example 7-3

Continuing with our previous example, how much will THH's EPS increase if the company's sales increase by 10 percent?

Answer:

$$DTL = DOL \times DFL = 2 \times 1.38 = 2.76$$

$$\frac{\Delta EPS}{EPS} = \frac{\Delta Q}{Q} \times DTL = 0.1 \times 2.76 = 27.6\%$$

7.1.4 Financial Risk and Financial Leverage

Financial risk refers to the additional risk that common stockholders have to bear as the firm increases the use of debt and preferred stock as sources of financing. As you will see shortly, the degree to which a firm uses fixed income financing is measured using a concept referred to as financial leverage. We shall also see that as a firm's financial leverage increases, earnings per share become more sensitive to changes in sales. So far, our discussion suggests that as financial leverage increases, the expected rate of return will increase, but at the cost of increased risk. This trade-off in using debt raises two related questions. Firstly, is the higher expected rate of return associated with debt sufficient to compensate for the increased risk? Secondly, what is the optimal amount of debt? The answers to both questions are essentially the same. That is, if the issuance of debt increases the value of the firm, then debt should be used, and the debt ratio that maximizes the firm's value is the optimal capital structure.

7.2 Capital Structure and Cost of Capital

The primary reason for studying weighted average cost of capital (WACC) is that the value of a firm is maximized when the WACC is minimized. WACC is the discount rate that is appropriate for the firm's overall cash flow. Since values and discount rates move in opposite directions, minimizing WACC will maximize the value of the firm's cash flow.

Thus, financial managers will choose a firm's capital structure so that the WACC is minimized. For this reason, we will say that one capital structure is better than another if it results in a lower WACC. Further, we say that a particular debt/equity ratio represents the optimal capital structure if it results in the lowest possible WACC. This is sometimes called a firm's optimal capital structure.

7.3 Capital Structure Theory

In 1958, Professors France Modigliani and Merton Miller (MM) published their seminal work on capital structure theory. MM proved, under a very restrictive set of assumptions, that a firm's value is unaffected by its capital structure. In other words, MM's results suggest that it does not matter how a firm finances its operations, so capital structure is irrelevant. Their results are based on the following simplifying assumptions.

- There are no transaction costs.
- Taxes are nonexistent.
- There is no cost of bankruptcy.
- Investors and corporations borrow at the same rate.
- Investors and managers have the same information about the future investment opportunities of a firm. This is called symmetric information.
- Debt has no effect on EBIT.

In the MM no tax world, the value of a firm is based on the value of the firm's assets. It has become common to explain the MM proposition in terms of a pie. That is, the size (value) of the pie (firm) does not depend on how it is sliced (the capital structure). The size of the pie depends on the size of the pie pan (the firm's asset base). So, with a given pie pan, the value of the firm's assets will be the same no matter how the firm finances (slices) it. This means that under the assumptions of perfect markets, the firm's WACC is constant, and the firm's capital structure does not influence the total value of the firm.

(1) The effect of taxes. In a subsequent paper, MM relaxed the assumption of no corporate taxes. Under the U.S. tax code, firms can deduct interest payments as an expense, while dividends are not an allowable expense when determining taxable income. This differential tax treatment encourages the corporate use of debt. The more the firm borrows, the greater the tax benefits that will accrue to the remaining stockholders. MM demonstrate that if their other assumptions hold, the optimal capital structure in a tax world will be 100 percent debts.

(2) The effect of bankruptcy costs. Relaxing MM's assumptions even more by introducing bankruptcy costs changes the analysis. Bankruptcy costs come from several sources. A firm in bankruptcy will have legal costs, added accounting costs, and may have to liquidate assets at low prices. Additionally, employees may leave, suppliers may refuse to ship except when cash payment is made, and customers may be lost. These costs may be incurred not only by a firm in bankruptcy, but also by a firm that is financially unsound and may go into bankruptcy. In

this case we term these costs the costs of financial distress.

The probability of bankruptcy (or even just costly financial distress), times bankruptcy costs is the expected cost of bankruptcy. Since firms with greater financial leverage are more likely to find themselves in bankruptcy or financial distress, expected bankruptcy costs increase with greater leverage and tend to decrease the value of the firm. This changes the relation between leverage and firm value. At low levels of debt, firm value increases when more debts are used in the capital structure. The existence of expected costs of bankruptcy at first slows this increase in firm value as more leverage is employed, and then decreases firm value as debt levels rise above some optimal amount.

7.4 Factors that Influence a Firm's Capital Structure Decision

● Business Risk: This is the risk that is inherent to a firm's basic operations in the absence of debt. The greater a firm's business risk, the lower its optimal debt ratio.

● Firm's tax exposure: One of the reasons for using debt is the tax deductibility of interest payments. The tax deductibility of interest lowers the effective cost of using debt. You should note, however, that when a firm already has a low tax rate because its income is sheltered from taxes by depreciation, interest on current debt or tax loss carries forward, and any additional debt will not be as advantageous as it would be to firms with higher effective tax rates.

● Financial flexibility: This refers to a firm's ability to go to the capital markets during adverse times and raise funds on reasonable terms. Lower debt levels provide more financial flexibility.

● Conservatism or aggressiveness of management: Firms with aggressive managers are more inclined to use debt in an effort to boost profits.

7.5 Features of an Optimal Capital Structure

● Profitability: A firm should make maximum use of leverage at minimum cost.

● Flexibility: It should be flexible enough to adapt to changing conditions. It should be in a position to raise funds in the shortest possible time and also repay the money borrowed, if it appears to be expensive. This is possible only if the company's lenders have not put forth any conditions like restricting the company from taking further loans, no restrictions placed on the assets usage or laying a restriction on early repayments. In other words, the finance authorities should have the power to take decisions on the basis of the circumstances.

- Control: The structure should have minimum dilution of control.
- Solvency: Use of excessive debt threatens the very existence of a company. Additional debt involves huge repayments. Loans with high interest rates are to be avoided however attractive some investment proposals might be. Some companies resort to the issuing of equity shares to repay their debt for equity holders that do not have a fixed rate of dividend.

7.6 Value of a Firm and Cost of Capital

value of a firm is calculated by estimating its future cash flow and then discounting this at the cost of capital. For the sake of simplification we will assume, in the following theoretical discussion, the future cash flow is constant and perpetual, and thus value of a firm is:

$$V = \frac{C}{\text{WACC}}$$

Where: V = value of a firm;

C = cash flow to be received one year here;

WACC = weighted average cost of capital.

The same logic can be applied to cash flow which is increasing at a constant rate, or which varies in an irregular fashion. The crucial point is this: if the cash flow is assumed to be at a set level then the value of a firm depends on the rate used to discount that cash flow. If the cost of capital is lowered, the value of a firm is raised.

What is meant by the value of a firm, V, is the combination of the market value of equity capital, V_E, plus the market value of debt capital, V_D.

$$V = V_E + V_D$$

Core Words

capital structure	资本结构
leverage	杠杆
operating leverage	经营杠杆
variable cost	变动成本
degree of operating leverage (DOL)	经营杠杆系数

financial leverage	财务杠杆
preferred stock	优先股
fixed cost	固定成本
degree of financial leverage (DFL)	财务杠杆系数
total leverage	总杠杆
degree of total leverage (DTL)	总杠杆系数
assumption	假设；假定
transaction cost	交易成本
bankruptcy	破产
financial distress	财务困境；财务危机
solvency	偿付能力；偿债能力
optimal capital structure	最佳资本结构

Key Concepts

1. Financial risk is the increased variability of EPS and increased risk of bankruptcy from greater financial leverage.

2. Operating leverage can be estimated as $\dfrac{Q(P-V)}{Q(P-V)-F}$ and interpreted as $\dfrac{Q(P-V)}{\text{EBIT}}$. Increases in operating leverage increase the variability of EBIT and EPS, increasing risk.

3. Financial leverage is the extent to which debt is used in the capital structure. Greater leverage increases financial risk, both the probability of default on debt (increasing the cost of debt) and the variability of EPS (increasing the cost of equity).

4. Adding debt to a firm's financing will increase expected earning per share and initially increase a firm's stock price. At some level of debt (optimal level), the increasing risk from more debt financing outweighs the increase in expected EPS, and the value of the firm will fall as more debt is used.

5. The value of a firm includes not only the value of the common stock (equity) but also the value of the debt.

6. Optimal capital structure is the proportion of debt and equity that minimizes the cost of financing (WACC) and thereby maximizes the value of a firm and shareholders' wealth (share price).

7. Four factors influence a firm's capital structure decision:
- Business risk.
- Firm's tax exposure.
- Financial flexibility.
- The conservatism or aggressiveness of management.

8. Under the MM assumptions of no taxes, transactions, or bankruptcy cost, the value of a firm and WACC are unaffected by leverage changes. Capital structure is irrelevant.

9. When taxes and bankruptcy costs are considered, there is a trade-off between the tax savings of increased debt (increasing firm value) and the increased bankruptcy risk of increased debt (decreasing firm value) so that there is an optimal debt level that maximizes the firm's value.

Extended Reading

资本结构理论发展路径

从纵向的历史维度看,基本上可以将资本结构理论分为旧资本结构理论与新资本结构理论。旧资本结构理论包括早期资本结构理论(1952—1958年)和传统资本结构理论(1958—1977年);新资本结构理论分为以代理成本模型和信息不对称模型为主的现代资本结构理论(20世纪70年代后期—80年代),以及其他的新资本结构理论(20世纪80年代至今)。其中,对于新的资本结构理论,如Milton Harris 和 Artur RAV(1991)在其回顾性文献中所综述的那样,由"以资本结构由什么决定为基础的模型群"构成。各阶段主要研究角度与代表观点如下表7-1所示。

表7-1 资本结构理论发展脉络

理论阶段	主要理论	代表人物	研究角度	主要观点
早期资本结构理论(1952—1958年)	净收入理论	David Durand (1952)	综合资本成本(WACC)	负债比率越高,企业价值越大
	净营业收入理论		综合资本成本(WACC)	企业价值不随负债比例变化
	传统理论		综合资本成本(WACC)	适度负债时企业价值最大

(续表)

理论阶段	主要理论		代表人物	研究角度	主要观点
传统资本结构理论(1958—1977年)	MM理论	MM无关理论	Modigliani 和 Miller (1958)	完美市场、套利理论	企业价值与资本结构无关
		修正MM理论	Modigliani 和 Miller (1963)	企业所得税、利息抵税	负债比例越高,企业价值越大
		米勒模型	Miller (1977)	企业所得税、个人所得税	负债比例越高,企业价值越大
	权衡理论	早期权衡理论	Scott 和 Myers	引入破产成本	最佳资本结构是权衡债务税盾与破产成本的结果
		后期权衡理论	Deangelo 和 Masulis	破产成本拓展为代理成本与财务困境成本	最佳资本结构是权衡债务税盾与代理成本、破产成本的结果
现代资本结构理论(20世纪70年代末—80年代)	代理成本理论		Jensen 和 Meckling (1976)	股权代理成本、债务代理成本	最佳资本成本是使代理成本最小的负债比率
	信号理论	Ross 模型	Ross (1977)	经营者内部信息	高负债传递利好信号
		风险厌恶模型	Leland 和 Pyle (1977)	经营者风险厌恶	管理者股份越高,越传递良好信号
		融资优序理论	Myers 和 Majluf	信息不对称,股票价值低估	股权融资被认为是不好的信号,企业融资遵循内源、债权、股权的先后顺序
其他新资本结构理论(20世纪80年代至今)	控制权理论		Aghion 和 Bolton, Haarris 和 Raviv 等	契约设计、控制权市场	通过金融合约设计,分配与转移企业控制权,并对企业价值产生影响
	产业组织理论		Brander、Lewis 和 Maksimovic 等	产业组织理论、产品竞争战略	资本结构受产品特征、产品市场、公司战略、资本市场等因素的影响
	行为金融理论		Stein、Baker 和 Wurgler	有限理性假设	存在适合公司发行新股的"市场时机",资本结构是"择时"的结果

资料来源:王斌.公司财务理论【M】.北京:清华大学出版社,2015.

Capital Structure

Questions and Problems

Choose the best answer to the following questions.

1. Which of the following statements is TRUE? The optimal capital structure (   ).

   A. minimizes the weighted average cost of capital (WACC) and maximizes the share price

   B. minimizes the cost of equity and maximizes the WACC

   C. minimizes the cost of debt, the cost of equity and the WACC

   D. is found by determining the debt-equity mix that maximizes expected earnings per share (EPS)

2. A firm's target capital structure is consistent with which of the following? (   )

   A. Minimum risk.   B. Minimum cost of equity.

   C. Maximum EPS.   D. Minimum WACC.

3. Which of the following is a key determinant of operating leverage? (   )

   A. The firm's beta.

   B. Level and cost of debt.

   C. The competitive nature of the business.

   D. The trade-off between fixed and variable costs.

4. Which of the following statements about capital structure and leverage is true? (   )

   A. Financial leverage is directly related to operating leverage.

   B. Increasing the corporate tax rate will not affect capital structure decisions.

   C. A firm with low operating leverage has a small proportion of its total costs in fixed costs.

   D. A firm with high business risk is more likely to increase its use of financial leverage than a firm with low business risk.

5. If JOC Inc. increases sales by 10 percent, JOC's EBIT increases by 15 percent. If JOC Inc. increases EBIT by 10 percent, EPS increases by 12 percent.

   (1) What is JOC's degree of operating leverage? (   )
   A. 1.2   B. 1.5   C. 1.8   D. 2.0

   (2) What is JOC's degree of financial leverage? (   )
   A. 1.2   B. 1.5   C. 1.8   D. 2.0

   (3) What is JOC's degree of total leverage? (   )
   A. 1.2   B. 1.5   C. 1.8   D. 2.0

6. JOC Inc. sells 10,000 units at a price of $5 per unit. JOC's fixed costs are $8,000,

interest expense is $2,000, variable costs are $3 per unit, and EBIT is $12,000.

    (1) What is JOC's degree of operating leverage? (　　)

    A. 1.25　　　　B. 1.50　　　　C. 1.67　　　　D. 1.75

    (2) What is JOC's degree of financial leverage? (　　)

    A. 1.00　　　　B. 1.20　　　　C. 1.33　　　　D. 1.67

    (3) What is JOC's degree of total leverage? (　　)

    A. 1.25　　　　B. 1.50　　　　C. 1.75　　　　D. 2.00

Short answer questions.

1. Explain the term operation leverage, financial leverage and total leverage.

2. What are business risk and financial risk?

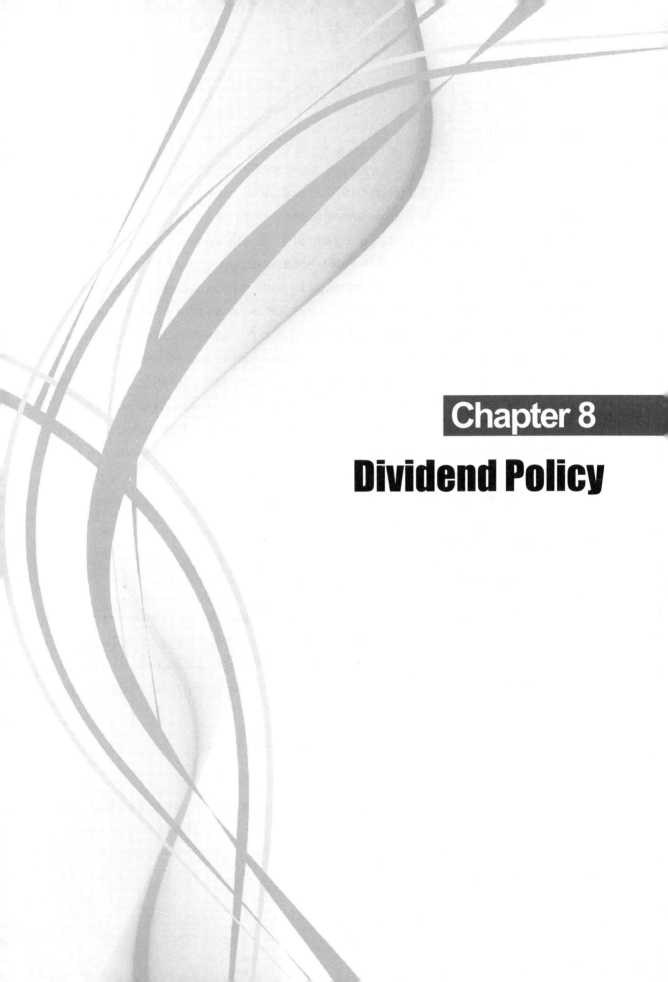

Chapter 8
Dividend Policy

Introduction

Apple Inc. which was founded in 1976, is a world famous public company. It paid out its cash dividends at $0.12 per share firstly in 1987, 7 years since it had gone public. Meanwhile it split its shares at a ratio of 1 : 2. The price per share increased by $1.75 on the declaration date of the split. Apple kept paying cash dividends around $0.45 per share stably until 1995 even though its performance decreased heavily from 1990 to 1995. It stopped paying dividends in 1996 because of a $742 million loss. Apple restarted paying cash dividends in 2012 due to the appeal to investors. What is the dividend policy for Apple? And what can we learn from its dividend policy?

Dividends are one of significant factors in corporate operating. There are two options a firm can choose when it makes profit: one is to pay dividends out to shareholders; another is to keep the profit in the firm, which is called retained earnings. Whether to pay dividends or not and how to pay the dividends are key points for a firm to decide. This chapter will introduce relative concepts regarding dividends and dividend policy.

8.1 Dividend Payments

8.1.1 Dividend

Dividend is the payment made to shareholders, which comes from a company's operating in the past financial year. It is the return to shareholders. Dividends can only be paid out from profit but not from capital, which can be paid in cash or other forms. Although there is no legal obligation for firms to pay shareholders dividends, the payment of dividends should comply with the laws.

8.1.2 Cash Dividend, Stock Dividend and Stock Split

1. Cash Dividends

If dividends are paid in cash, it is normally from the corporation's current earnings and accumulated profits. Paying cash dividends will change its financial statement as a result of decrease in both current asset and current liability. The shareholders' equity with cash dividends does not move.

2. Stock Dividends

For stock dividends, the payment is made in the form of additional shares rather than a cash payout. If dividends are paid in cash, those dividends are taxable leading to an increase in tax of shareholders. When a company pays share dividends instead of cash, there are usually no tax consequences for shareholders until the stock is sold. Paying stock dividends only transfers the internal structures of owners' equity. The total amount of shareholders' equity is not changed.

Example 8-1

THK Inc. firm plans to pay 10% stock dividends. And the current market price is $5 per share. The changes of equity before and after dividends payout are show in below Table 8-1 and 8-2.

Table 8-1 Before the stock dividends

Common stock	
Face value (1 million share, $2/share)	$2,000,000
Capital surplus	$8,000,000
Retained earnings	$12,000,000
Shareholders' equity	$22,000,000

Table 8-2 After the stock dividends

Common stock	
Face value (1 million share, $2/share)	$2,200,000
Capital surplus	$8,300,000
Retained earnings	$11,500,000
Shareholders' equity	$22,000,000

A firm may decide to distribute the stock dividends to shareholders of record if the firm's availability of liquid cash is insufficient or the company in tends to keep cash for future reinvestment.

3. Stock Split

Stock split is a corporate action in which a firm divides its existing shares into multiple shares. It leads to an increase in the number of shares outstanding. However, the total value of shares maintains the same, as no real value is added as a consequence of the split.

For the stockholders, there is no change in their wealth if a company makes a stock split. For the senior managers, the stock split can reduce the market price of shares, making it easier for more investors to trade the stocks. Additionally, it can be regarded as a preparation for a new stocks issue. Furthermore, it can support a company to make mergers and acquisitions (M&A) decisions.

8.1.3 Dividends Payment

Dividend policy must be declared by the board of directors (BOD). Four important dates are listed below during the dividends payout procedure.

● The declaration (or announcement) date: on the declaration date the board of directors meets and makes an announcement about how much the regular dividend will be. At this point, the total amount to be paid is transferred from retained earnings to an accrued liability in the firm's financial statements.

● The record (or holder of record) date: holder of record is the person who officially owns a share or shares on a given date. At the close of business on this day, the company draws up a list of its shareholders. Only shareholders who appear on this list are entitled to receive the dividends. If the stocks are traded but the change of ownership are not on the stock transfer book on this date, then the previous owner can obtain the dividend.

● The ex-dividend date: in order to avoid potential problems associated with changes in ownership of shares close to the record date, the ex-dividend date is set. It is always 3 days before the record date. Any investor buying the shares before the date will receive the dividends announced. While anyone buying the shares on or after the ex-dividend date is not entitled to get the dividends.

● The payment date: this is the day on which the dividend is actually paid to the shareholders, generally two months after the ex-dividend date. The economic benefit will actually flow out of the firm and corporate repays the liabilities related to the dividends.

8.2 Overview of Dividend Policy

8.2.1 Factors Affecting Dividend Policy

Dividend policy is the decision made by a firm to pay out earning versus retaining and reinvesting them. Several factors must be considered when a firm establishes its dividend policy.

● The liquidity position of a firm: this is because a profit gained does not mean that the firm has enough cash.

● The rate of asset expansion: the greater the rate of expansion of a firm, the greater the retained earning required to finance. This is because the cost of retained earnings is usually lower than the cost of stock with lower financial risk.

● The shareholders: paying dividends, to some extent, may make stockholders confident in a firm. Additionally, as we have mentioned above, different types of dividends may lead to different tax payments for shareholders. Therefore, the interest of shareholders should be considered when the firm makes its dividend policy.

- Legal consideration: a firm's dividend policy must abide by the legislations and codes.

8.2.2 Residual Policy

The dividend paid by a firm comes after satisfying its investment required, meanwhile the target capital structure should be maintained within this dividend policy. The shareholders may prefer to retain the earnings in the firm instead of a dividend payout.

Using this model is a four steps process:

- Determine the optimal capital budget.
- Determine the amount of equity needed to finance this budget, given the firms target capital structure.
- Use retained earnings to fund as much of the budget as possible.
- Pay dividends only if there are earnings left over after meeting the financing requirements for the optimal capital budget.

The dividend payout ratio can be calculated as:

$$Dividend\ payout\ ratio = \frac{Total\ paid\ as\ dividends}{Net\ income}$$

Example 8-2

THK Inc. has $1.8 million in available earnings. It needs $1.6 million to fund a new investment and the target equity ratio is 50%.

Requirement: how much in dividends will be paid and what is the dividend payout ratio?

Solution:

Equity needed = 1.6 × 50% = $0.8 million

Dividend paid = 1.8 − 0.8 = $1 million

Dividend payout ratio = 1 ÷ 1.8 = 55.56%

The residual policy can maintain capital structure and minimize new stock issues and flotation costs, hence, it, to some extent, minimizes the WACC. However, it may result in variable dividends and risk increasing.

8.2.3 Constant Dividend Payout Ratio

With this policy, a company will pay a fixed percentage of net earnings to shareholders. Establishing this policy, the dividends may be variable and unpredicted as the float of net profit. This may affect the confidence of shareholders in the company.

8.2.4　Stable Dividend Policy

With this dividend policy, the dividend payment is steady and predictable each year, which is what most investors seek. Whether earnings are up or down, investors could receive a dividend. This policy reduces uncertainty for investors while increasing the financial pressure for companies. Companies following this policy are always attempting to share earnings with shareholders rather than searching for projects in which to invest excess cash.

8.3　Share Repurchase

Share repurchase is a kind of transaction in which a firm buys back its own outstanding stocks. The motivation of a share buyback can be:

- The firm has excess cash and aims to distribute to the shareholders by buying stock back instead of paying dividends. It is an alternative to distributing cash as dividends.
- The firm wants to change its capital structure as it has too much equity.
- It is a protection against a takeover of shareholders as the outstanding dividends decrease.

The share repurchase transfers a positive signal to investors that shares are undervalued, and it gives shareholders more choices. It may avoid setting a high for dividends that can not be maintained. Additionally, the share repurchase reduces the threat of being acquisitioned. However, the repurchase may be viewed as a negative signal that the firm has poor investment opportunities. Shareholders who sell in a buyback must be told of all the implications of their decision, or they might sue the company.

A dividend policy introduces how to calculate dividends and how to pay dividends. To establish a dividend policy, the corporate managers should consider both the company itself and its stakeholders. Appropriate dividend policy may have positive effects on the company.

Core Words

dividend policy	股利政策
dividend payment	股利支付
cash dividend	现金股利

stock dividend	股票股利
stock split	股票分割
declaration date	股利宣告日
record date	股权登记日
ex-dividend date	除息日
payment date	股利支付日
residual policy	剩余股利政策
capital budget	资本预算
capital structure	资本结构
dividend payout ratio	股利支付率
constant dividend payout ratio	固定股利支付率
stock repurchase	股票回购

Key Concepts

1. Dividend is the payment made to shareholders from operating earnings. It is the return for shareholders.

2. There are two types of dividends: cash dividends and stock dividends. The payment of each kind of dividends may have different effects on both the financial reports especially the balance sheet for the company and the benefits of shareholders.

3. There are four important dates: the declaration (or announcement) date, the record (or holder of record) date, the ex-dividend date and the payment date during the dividend payment procedure.

4. Liquidity position of a firm, rate of asset expansion, shareholders and legislation are the four factors that should be considered when a firm makes its dividend policy.

5. Residual policy is the policy that the dividend paid by a firm comes after satisfying the investment required within the firm's capital structure.

6. Share repurchase is a kind of transaction in which the firm buys back its own outstanding stock. It could protect against a takeover by shareholders. Additionally, it transfers a positive signal to investors that shares are undervalued, and it gives shareholders more choices.

Extended Reading

股利理论

当今主要的股利理论可以分成两类。一类是以MM理论为代表的股利无关论;另一类是股利相关论。

一、股利无关论

股利无关论,又称MM理论,该理论建立在完全市场理论之上,假定条件包括:①公司所有的股东均能准确地掌握公司的情况,对于将来的投资机会,投资者与管理者拥有相同的信息;②不存在任何公司或个人所得税;③不存在任何筹资费用(包括发行费用和各种交易费用);④公司的投资决策与股利决策彼此独立。该理论认为,在一定的假设条件限定下,股利政策不会对公司的价值或股票的价格产生任何影响。一家公司的股票价格完全由其投资决策的获利能力和风险组合决定,而与公司的利润分配政策无关。

二、股利相关论

股利相关论主要有"在手之鸟"理论、信号传递理论、所得税差异理论和代理理论。

1. "在手之鸟"理论

"在手之鸟"理论认为,用留存收益再投资给投资者带来的收益具有较大的不确定性,并且投资的风险随着时间的推移会进一步增大,因此,投资者更喜欢现金股利,而不愿意将收益留存在公司内部,去承担未来的投资风险。

2. 信号传递理论

信号传递理论认为,在信息不对称的情况下,公司可以通过股利政策向市场传递有关公司未来盈利能力的信息,从而影响公司的股价。一般来讲,预期未来盈利能力强的公司往往愿意通过相对较高的股利支付水平,把自己同预期盈利能力差的公司区别开来,以吸引更多的投资者。

3. 所得税差异理论

所得税差异理论认为,由于普遍存在的税率差异及纳税时间的差异,资本利得收入比股利收入更有助于实现收益最大化目标,企业应当采用低股利政策。

4. 代理理论

代理理论认为,股利政策有助于减缓管理者与股东之间的代理冲突,股利政策是协调股东与管理者之间代理关系的一种约束机制。较多地派发现金股利至少具有以下几点

Dividend Policy

好处：①公司管理者将公司的盈利以股利的形式支付给投资者，则管理者自身可以支配的"闲余现金流量"就相应减少了，这在一定程度上可以抑制公司管理者过度扩大投资或进行特权消费，从而保护外部投资者的利益；②较多地派发现金股利，减少了内部融资，导致公司进入资本市场寻求外部融资，从而使公司可以接受资本市场的有效监督，这样便可以通过资本市场的监督减少代理成本。

Questions and Problems

Choose the best answer to the following questions.

1. Dividend policy of a company is declared by (　　).

A. the board of directors.

B. the shareholders.

C. the debt holders.

D. the securities exchange.

2. Paying out the cash dividends will (　　).

A. increase the total equity.

B. decrease the total equity.

C. not affect an equity.

D. change the inside structure of equity.

3. ACC Inc. has decided on a 3-for-1 stock split. If the firm currently has $w1,800,000 shares outstanding, how many shares will be outstanding after the stock split? (　　)

A. 600,000 shares.

B. 2,400,000 shares.

C. 3,200,000 shares.

D. 3,600,000 shares.

4. (　　) is the date when the board of directors announce the next dividend to the public.

A. Declaration date.

B. Record date.

C. Payment date.

D. Ex-dividend date.

5. Residual dividend policy is the one in which(   ).

A. left over funds are paid out to stockholders as dividends after all other capital requirements are met within the required capital structure.

B. a stable dividend payment is made each period to stockholders.

C. dividends will be paid that are not given the investment opportunity.

D. dividends will be paid that are not given the capital structure.

6. BC firm has $2.5 million in available earnings. It needs $3 million to fund a new investment and the target equity ratio is 60%. How much dividends should be paid? (   )

A. $0.7 million.

B. $1.3 million.

C. $0 million.

D. $2.5 million.

7. When a company applies the constant dividend payout ratio policy, the dividends (   ).

A. will be paid steady forever.

B. will be paid at a stable payout ratio.

C. are not relating to the performance of the company.

D. all the above.

8. Stock repurchase is generally considered by the market to be (   ).

A. good news.

B. bad news.

C. not newsworthy.

D. no answer.

9. Which of the following is the reason for a company to repurchase its shares? (   )

A. The company has excess cash.

B. The company wants to change its capital structure.

C. The company wishes protection against a takeover by shareholders.

D. All the above.

10. Which of the following statements is not correct? (   )

A. Stock split sends good news to investors.

B. The liquidity position of a firm should be taken into account when making the dividend policy.

C. Investors buying shares before the ex-dividend date will receive the dividends announced.

D. The payment of stock dividends will increase the total amount of equity.

Short answer questions.

1. What factors should be considered when establishing dividend policy?
2. What are the advantages and disadvantages of residual policy?
3. What are the advantages and disadvantages of share repurchase?

Part IV

Valuation

Chapter 9

Introduction to Asset Valuation

Introduction to Asset Valuation — Chapter 9

Introduction

Smith, a milk products company, owns a 1800km^2 farm located in South Island of New Zealand. There is a 4000m^2 house and 5000 cows on the farm. Now, it aims to dispose of the farm as its business scope is adjusted. Smith entrusts SK asset valuation firm to evaluate the farm. It receives the result — the valuation report after 15 days. Based on the report, Smith makes a reasonable pricing decision and sells the farm successfully.

Every asset, whether physical or not, has a value. Understanding what the value is has become one of the key points of corporate operating. This chapter will explain some concepts of asset valuation, together with the assumptions, process and approaches of asset appraisal.

9.1 Asset Valuation

9.1.1 Definition of Asset Valuation

Asset valuation refers to the act and process by which an asset appraiser, in accordance with the relevant laws, regulations and asset valuation standards, analyzes and estimates the assets value for specific purposes on the valuation date, and issues professional opinions. Asset appraisal is composed of 10 basic elements:

- Valuation subject: the institutions and personnel engaged in asset valuation, including legal entities and individuals.
- Valuation object: the asset to be valued.
- Valuation basis: the laws and regulations that must be complied with during the process of asset valuation.
- Valuation purpose: the reason for asset valuation, depending on the requirements of the client.
- Valuation principles: the codes that must be followed during the asset valuation.
- Valuation procedures: the systematic steps of asset valuation.
- Type of value: the attribute value of asset appraisal result and its form of expression, which depends on the valuation purpose accordingly.
- Valuation approaches: the means and techniques that should be applied in asset valuation.

● Valuation assumptions: the inferences based on the facts and its reasonable trend during the valuation process. It is the precondition of valuation consequence.

● Valuation date: the date on which the estimate of value applies. This may be different from the date on which the valuation report is to be issued or the date on which investigations are to be undertaken or completed.

9.1.2 Characteristics of Asset Valuation

1. Marketability

Asset valuation should satisfy the demands of market and valuation result should be accepted by the market test.

2. Impartiality

The processes of asset valuation, including assessment procedures, principles and conclusion should be impartial. The assessment staff should be an independent third party that is not a stakeholder in the valuation target.

3. Independence

Both the valuation institution and asset appraisers should make an independent judgment of the value of assets. During the whole process, they are not affected by the clients and any other personnel or intuitions.

4. Specialty

The valuation institution and staff should be professional. This has two aspects. On the one hand, asset valuation institutions are composed of experts and professors in this field. On the other hand, the estimate of the asset by the appraisers is made on the basis of professional knowledge and experience.

5. Advisory

The consequence of valuation is not mandatory, but advisory. It supports the clients to make decisions regarding the price of the assets.

9.2 Assumptions of Asset Valuation

9.2.1 Open Market Concepts

Open market is the competitive market where the participants are acting freely. The market for assets can be a regional market, a domestic market or an international market, which consists of numerous buyers and sellers. The trade in the market is voluntary and rational, without being mandatory or having limitations. Asset value of trade, in an open market, is determined by the market rather than individual trade opinion.

9.2.2 Continue to Use Concepts

This hypothesis describes the existent state of an asset. It sets that the asset is in use, and that it will continue to be in use. The assets include the asset in use and the spare.

9.2.3 Liquidation Concepts

Liquidation illustrates the fact that asset is facing liquidation or will possibly be liquidated in the future. Under this assumption, the transaction is compulsory and time limited. The sides of exchange are unequal. The assessment value is lower than the estimate value under open market or continue to use hypotheses.

9.3 Types of Value

The types of value are numerous. Different types of value can express the property and features from different sides. This book emphasizes on four types of value: market value, replacement value, present value and liquidation value.

9.3.1 Market Value

Market value is the estimated value in an arm's length transaction on the valuation date. Both parties of the exchange should act intelligently, prudently, and without compulsion.

9.3.2 Replacement Cost

Replacement cost or replacement value refers to the actual cost of replacing an asset at the present time, according to its current worth.

9.3.3 Present Value

The present value refers to the discount value of future cash flows. It is focused on the future cash flows or income achieved by specific assets.

9.3.4 Liquidation Value

Liquidation value is the price of an asset when the entity is dissolved. Liquidation value is typically lower than the market value.

9.4 Procedures of Asset Valuation

Procedures of asset valuation are the systematic steps of valuation organizations and asset appraisers perform during the assessment. The main steps are listed as follow:

Step 1 — clarify the basic matters of asset valuation.

Step 2 — make an agreement of asset valuation.

Step 3 — draw up the plans of asset valuation.

Step 4 — field investigation of assets.

Step 5 — collect references for asset valuation.

Step 6 — estimation and assessment.

Step 7 — work out and submit the report of asset valuation.

Step 8 — file the working paper of asset valuation.

9.5 Approaches of Asset Valuation

One or more valuation approaches may be used in order to achieve the valuation of assets. The three approaches described and defined in this chapter are the main approaches used in valuation. They are all based on the economic principles of price equilibrium, anticipation of benefits or substitution.

9.5.1 Market Approach

1. Basis of market approach

The market approach estimates value by comparison between the subject asset and the prices of identical or similar assets. The idea underlying this method is that similar assets should sell at similar prices.

It can be used to obtain estimates of value quickly for assets, and is particularly useful when a large number of comparable assets are traded on the open market.

$$Value\ of\ asset = Transaction\ price\ of\ reference \times \frac{Comparable\ characteristics\ value\ of\ asset}{Comparable\ characteristics\ value\ of\ reference}$$

2. Understanding market approach

Under this approach, the first step is to consider the prices for transactions of identical or similar assets, called references, that have occurred recently in the open market.

Finding comparable and similar assets is often a challenge. If few recent transactions of the target asset have occurred, it may also be appropriate to consider the prices of identical or similar assets that are listed or offered for sale. These prices of reference are clearly established and critically analyzed in the open market providing relevant information. It is necessary to adjust the price information from other transactions to reflect any differences in terms of the actual transaction and the basis of value and any assumptions to be adopted in the valuation being undertaken. There may also be differences in the legal, economic or physical characteristics of the assets in other transactions and the asset being valued.

One could choose appropriate comparable characteristics of references and assets being valued when estimating the value of assets, according to the different characteristics of different kinds of assets.

Three or more references should be selected, as the prices of references are not only affected by the characteristics of assets themselves, such as their function, quality and so on; but also by the condition of the market and transactions including the relationship between demand and supply, the intentions and dates of transactions and others. The value of an asset is the average of adjusted value from references.

Example 9-1

EK valuation institution is required to evaluate an apartment YH. In order to value YH, the appraisers find 3 comparable apartments Y, Z, A in the market. The market value of them is $900 thousand, $890 thousand and $895 thousand respectively. Appraisers give scores on the living environment of the 4 apartments. The scores are 9, 8, 9.5, 8.5 for Y, Z, YH, A respectively.

Requirement: estimate the value of YH.

Solution:

Value of YH by adjusting Y = $900 \times \frac{9.5}{9}$ = $950 thousand

Value of YH by adjusting Z = $890 \times \frac{9.5}{8}$ = $1,056.88 thousand

Value of YH by adjusting A = $895 \times \frac{9.5}{8.5}$ = $1,000.29 thousand

Value of YH = $(950+1056.88+1000.29) \div 3$ = $1,002.39 thousand

9.5.2 Income Approach

1. Basis of Income Approach

The income approach estimates value by converting future cash flows to a single current capital value applying either discounted cash flow techniques. In simple cases, it is the application of a capitalization multiple to a representative single period cash flow. The value is determined by cash flows or cost savings generated by the asset, useful life of asset and discount rate or capitalization rate reflecting the riskiness of the estimated cash flows.

$$Value\ of\ asset = \sum_{t=1}^{n} \frac{CF_t}{(1+r)^t}$$

Where: t = useful life of asset;

CF_t = cash flow referring to profit at period t;

r = discount rate or capitalization rate reflecting the riskiness of the estimated cash flows.

2. Understanding of Income Approach

This approach considers the income or cash flows that an asset will generate over its useful life and estimates value through a capitalization process. Capitalization involves the conversion of income into a capital sum through the application of an appropriate discount rate. The income stream may be derived under contract or not, and the anticipated profit generated from either holding or use of the asset.

Methods that fall under the income approach include:

- Income capitalization, where an all risks or overall capitalization rate is applied to a representative single period income.
- Discounted cash flow where a discount rate is applied to a series of cash flows for future periods to discount them to a present value.
- Various option pricing models.

To apply this method, three conditions should be satisfied:

- Future income or cash flows could be forecasted and measured by currency. Income or cash flows can be identified for the asset or the group of assets in asset valuation. It is future economic benefits, not the historical or present. And it is objective not actual.
- The risk of future income for asset holders could be forecasted and measured. Factors such as the level of interest rates, rates of return and the risk inherent in the anticipated benefit stream should be considered in estimating the appropriate discount rate. The capitalization rate refers to the discount rate when the future income is perpetual. It should be mentioned that the capitalization or discount rate applied must be consistent with the definition of income or cash flows used.
- The period of income, which refers to the useful life, could be forecast. And the useful life is usually measured in years.

The income approach can be applied to liabilities by considering the cash flows required to service a liability until it is discharged.

> ***Example 9-2***
>
> THC Inc. plans to invest in a profitable asset and the income of the asset should be predicted. It estimates that THC will obtain $130,000, $150,000, $160,000, $110,000 and $140,000 in the first 5 years and the income will remain at $140,000 per year from the 6th year. The discount rate is 10%.
>
> **Requirement:** estimate the value of the asset.
>
> **Solution:**
> $$\text{PV of first 5 years} = \frac{130,000}{(1+10\%)} + \frac{150,000}{(1+10\%)^2} + \frac{160,000}{(1+10\%)^3} + \frac{110,000}{(1+10\%)^4} + \frac{140,000}{(1+10\%)^5}$$
> $$= 130,000 \times 0.9091 + 150,000 \times 0.8264 + 160,000 \times 0.7513$$
> $$+ 110,000 \times 0.6830 + 140,000 \times 0.6209$$
> $$= \$524,407$$
> $$\text{Value of asset} = 524,407 + \frac{140,000}{10\%} \times \frac{1}{(1+10\%)^5} = 524,407 + 869,260 = \$1,393,667$$

9.5.3 Cost Approach

1. Basis of Cost Approach

The cost approach estimates value using the economic principle that a buyer will pay no more for an asset than the cost to obtain an asset of equal utility, whether by purchase or by construction.

Value of asset = Replacement cost of asset – Cost deductions

2. Understanding Cost Approach

This approach is based on the economic principle that the price that a buyer in the market would pay for the asset being valued would be no more than the cost to purchase or construct a modern equivalent asset excluding unusual situations. The asset being valued will always be less attractive than the alternative that could be purchased or constructed because of age or obsolescence. As a result, adjustments will need to be made to the cost of the alternative asset.

The cost approach is commonly adopted for tangible assets particularly in the case of individual assets or a group of assets that are specialized. The asset's value is the depreciated replacement cost of it. The replacement cost is the cost of obtaining an alternative asset of equivalent utility. The alternative can either be a similar asset providing the same or similar functionality or an exact replica of the subject asset. The latter is only appropriate where the cost of a replica would be less than the cost of a similar asset or where only a replica rather than a similar asset could provide the same utility of the subject asset.

(1) Replacement cost

One or more methods, such as a replacement algorithm, price index method and so on, may be used to arrive at estimating replacement cost. This book will focus on the method of a replacement algorithm. The replacement cost needs to reflect all incidental costs. For purchase items, the replacement cost includes purchase price, freight, installation costs and other necessary costs. For constructed items, construction cost, necessary finance cost and reasonable profit of developers should be taken into consideration.

Example 9-3

THC Inc. wants to construct a set of equipment. The direct construction cost is $200,000. In order to construct the equipment, THC borrows a one-year loan from ABC bank. The amount is $100,000, and the interest is 5% per year.

Requirement: estimate the replacement cost of the equipment.

Solution:

Finance cost = 100,000 × 5% = $5,000

Replacement cost = 200,000 + 5,000 = $205,000

(2) Cost deductions

Having established the replacement cost, deductions are made to reflect the physical, functional and economic obsolescence of the subject asset when compared to the alternative asset that could be acquired at the replacement cost.

Example 9-4

THC Inc. plans to purchase a set of second-hand manufactory equipment. Its market price, related delivery cost and direct installation cost are $100,000, $20,000 and $30,000 respectively. In addition, the indirect installation cost is 10% of the market price. The physical deduction and economic deductions related to the equipment are $10,000 and $25,000.

Requirement: estimate the value of the equipment.

Solution:

Direct cost = 100,000 + 20,000 + 30,000 = $150,000

Indirect cost = 100,000 × 10% = $10,000

Replacement cost = 150,000 + 10,000 = $160,000

Cost deduction = 10,000 + 25,000 = $35,000

Value of equipment = Replacement cost − Cost deduction = 160,000 − 35,000 = $125,000

Chapter 9
Introduction to Asset Valuation

Asset valuation is significant during the operation of enterprises. Appraisers should assess the assets in the appropriate forms of value following the asset valuation procedures, under certain assumptions. Based on the specific details of different kinds of assets, different valuation techniques are required to be used by asset appraisers. Selecting the appropriate method is a key point for asset appraisers, and they should mention the characteristics of assets during the process of valuation.

Core Words

asset valuation	资产评估
valuation subject	评估主体
valuation object	评估客体
valuation basis	评估依据
valuation purpose	评估目的
valuation principle	评估原则
valuation procedure	评估程序
type of value	价值类型
valuation approach	评估方法
valuation assumption	评估假设
valuation date	资产评估基准日
liquidation value	清算价值
open market assumption	公开市场假设
continue to use assumption	持续使用假设
liquidation assumption	清算假设
market value	市场价值
replacement cost	重置成本
liquidation value	清算价值
report of asset valuation	资产评估报告
working paper	工作底稿
market approach	市场法
reference	参照物
income approach	收益法
useful life of asset	使用寿命；收益期
capitalization rate	资本化率
cost deduction	资产贬值
physical deduction	实体性贬值
economic deduction	经济性贬值
functional deduction	功能性贬值

Key Concepts

1. Asset valuation refers to the act and process by which an asset appraiser, in accordance with the relevant laws, regulations and asset valuation standards, analyze and estimate the assets, value for specific purposes on the valuation date, and issue professional opinions.

2. There are ten basic elements for asset valuation: valuation subject, valuation object, valuation basis, valuation purpose, valuation principles, valuation procedures, type of value, valuation approaches, valuation assumptions and valuation date.

3. To understand asset valuation, the characteristics of asset valuation should be taken into consideration.

4. Assumptions are the preconditions for appraisers undertaking asset valuation. The appraisers should apply different assumptions for different valuation purposes.

5. Valuation approaches are the techniques for asset valuation. There are three main approaches being introduced.

- Market approach: estimates the value by comparison between the subject asset and the prices of references. Three or more references should be chosen to ensure accuracy in the consequent valuation.

- Cost approach: estimates the value by computing the replacement cost and deductions.

- Income approach: estimates the value by discounting future income to present. There are three factors that should be taken account: future income, discount rate and the period of asset use or holding.

Extended Reading

资产评估相关准则

为了使评估价值更加客观合理，相关国际组织、区域组织以及许多国家和地区的资产评估协会或者政府部门都制定了资产评估执业准则和职业道德规范等。例如国际评估准则理事会(International Valuation Standards Committee，IVSC)制定并努力推广《国际评估准则》(*International Valuation Standards*，*IVS*)，欧洲评估师协会联合会(The European

Group of Valuers' Associations，TEGoVA) 制定了《欧洲评估准则》(*European Valuation Standards, EVS*)，美国评估促进会评估准则委员会(The Appraisal Standards Board of The Appraisal Foundation) 制定了《美国评估准则》(*Uniform Standards of Professional Appraisal Practice，USPAP*)，英国皇家特许测量师学会(Royal Institution of Chartered Surveyors, RICS) 制定了《皇家特许测量师学会评估准则》(*RICS Valuation Standards*)。

资产评估报告

一、定义

资产评估报告是指注册资产评估师根据资产评估准则的要求，在履行了必要的评估程序后，对评估对象在评估基准日特定目的下的价值发表的，由其所在评估机构出具的书面专业意见。资产评估报告更多地是强调评估报告的形式和格式，即按照一定格式和内容来反映评估目的、假设、程序、标准、依据、方法、结果及适用条件等基本情况的报告书。

广义的资产评估报告还是一种工作制度。规定评估机构在完成评估工作之后必须按照一定程序的要求用书面形式报告评估过程和结果。而狭义的资产评估报告更多地关注其文字报告本身，它是资产评估机构履行评估合同的总结，同时也是资产评估主体为资产评估项目承担相应法律责任的书面证明。

《国际评估准则》(IVS)和《美国评估准则》(USPAP)对评估报告都是从报告类型和报告要素上进行规范的。我国2007年发布的《资产评估准则——评估报告》是根据要素与内容对评估报告进行规范的重要评估准则，2015年发布的《企业国有资产评估报告指南》则从国有资产评估报告的基本内容与格式方面对评估报告的标题、文号、声明、摘要、正文、附件、评估明细表和评估说明等进行了规范。中国资产评估协会根据《资产评估准则》于2017年和2018年分别对《企业国有资产评估报告指南》和《资产评估准则——评估报告》进行了修订。

二、种类

按照不同的分类标准，资产评估报告可分为如下几种。

(1) 按资产评估的范围可分为整体资产评估报告与单项资产评估报告

凡是对整体资产进行评估所出具的资产评估报告称为整体资产评估报告，凡是仅对某一部分、某一项资产进行评估所出具的资产评估报告称为单项资产评估报告。通常来说，前者不仅包括资产方面的还包括负债和所有者权益方面的列报，而后者更注重对某一部分或某一项资产方面的列报，除在建工程外，一般不考虑负债和以整体资产为依托的无形资产。

(2) 按国际惯例可分为完整型评估报告、简明型评估报告与限制型评估报告

完整型评估报告评估主体，即委托方，须向客户提供最详尽的信息；简明型评估报告仅对解决评估问题具有重要意义的信息作出概括说明；限制型评估报告仅供委托方使用，在提供限制性报告时，资产评估师应在报告中明确指出该报告的类型。这三种评估意见的根本区别在于所提供信息的详细程度不同。

(3) 按资产评估的性质可分为一般评估报告和复核评估报告

一般评估报告是指评估人员接受客户委托，为客户提供的关于资产价值的估价意见的书面报告，如完整型评估报告、简明型评估报告、限制型评估报告等。复核评估报告是指复核评估师对一般评估报告的充分性和合理性发表意见的书面报告，是复核评估师对一般评估报告进行评估和审核的报告。两种报告的编制者是不同的。

三、资产评估报告的作用

(1) 为被委托评估的资产提供作价意见

资产评估报告书是经具有资产评估资格的机构根据委托评估资产的特点和要求组织评估师及相应的专业人员组成的评估队伍，遵循评估原则和标准，按照法定的程序，运用科学的方法对被评估资产价值进行评定和估算后，通过报告书的形式提出作价的意见。该作价意见不代表任何当事人一方的利益，是一种独立专家估价的意见，具有较强的公正性与客观性，因而成为被委托评估资产作价的重要参考依据。

(2) 资产评估报告书是反映和体现资产评估工作情况，明确委托方、受托方及有关方面责任的依据

它以文字的形式，对受托资产评估业务的目的、背景、范围、依据、程序、方法等过程和评定的结果进行说明和总结，体现了评估机构的工作成果。同时，资产评估报告书也反映和体现了受托的资产评估机构与执业人员的权利与义务，并以此来明确委托方、受托方有关方面的法律责任。资产评估报告书也是评估机构履行评估协议和向委托方或有关方面收取评估费用的依据。

(3) 对资产评估报告书进行审核，是管理部门完善资产评估管理的重要手段

资产评估报告书是反映评估机构的评估人员职业道德、执业能力水平，以及评估质量高低和机构内部管理机制完善程度的重要依据。有关管理部门通过审核资产评估报告书，可以有效地对评估机构的业务开展情况进行监督和管理。

(4) 资产评估报告书是建立评估档案、归集评估档案资料的重要信息来源

评估机构和评估人员在完成资产评估任务之后，都必须按照档案管理的有关规定，将评估过程收集的资料、工作记录以及资产评估过程的有关工作底稿进行归档，以便进行评估档案的管理和使用。

资产评估方法

一、不同国家的基本评估方法

关于资产评估的基本方法,美国体系主要有成本法(cost approach)、市场比较法(market comparison approach, sales comparison approach)、收益法(income approach)三种;英国体系主要有比较法(comparison method, comparative method)、投资法(investment method)、剩余法(residual method)、利润法(profit method)四种。英国的比较法和美国的市场比较法与我国的市场法相同;英国的投资法和利润法可以归为收益法,剩余法可以归为成本法。从整体来看,不管是中国的还是外国的资产评估基本方法,其基本思想是一致的,只是在具体的评估细节方面存在一定的差异。

二、资产评估方法评价

1. 成本法

成本法是指首先估测被评估资产的重置成本,然后估测被评估资产业已存在的各种贬损因素,并将其从重置成本中予以扣除而得到被评估资产价值的各种评估方法的总称。成本法考虑的是资产的过去而不是未来。这种方法的优点是比较充分地考虑了资产的损耗,评估结果更趋于公平合理;在不易计算资产未来收益或难以取得市场参照物的条件下可以广泛地运用;有利于企业资产的保值。但成本法的应用也有一定的局限性。首先,成本法难以全面估算资产的经济性贬值。经济性贬值是指由于外部因素变化而导致资产价值的损失,是无形损耗的一种表现。这种经济性贬值往往是外部因素的变化对企业整体产生影响,进而影响到单项资产的使用。因此,对经济性贬值的估算实质上是对外部因素就企业整体获利能力影响的评估,对此,成本法无能为力。其次,采用成本法评估时无法评估出将资产组配成具有获利能力的整体性资产的创造性劳动价值,这种创造性的劳动价值最终通过整体性资产的获利能力表现出来,而成本法只能评估资产的购置成本。

2. 市场法

市场法考虑的是相同或类似资产的可替代性和市场价格反映资产内在价值的原理,比照相同或类似资产的市场价格来确定资产的价值。优点是评估参数和指标直接从市场获得,能客观反映资产目前的市场情况;评估值更能反映市场的实际价格,评估结果易于被各方面了解和接受。这种方法的缺点是:第一,前提严格,需要有公开活跃的市场,若缺少可对比数据或缺少判断对比数据则难以应用;第二,适用范围受限制,不适用于专用机器、设备、大部分的无形资产及受地区、环境等严格限制的一些资产的评估;第三,对价值比率的调整是运用市场法极为关键的一步,需要评估师具有丰富的实践经验和较强的技术能力。

3. 收益法

收益法考虑的是未来现金流量，与资产的过去、现在无关，资产之所以有价值，归根结底是由于其能给持有者带来未来收益，而未来收益是资产价值的源泉。这种方法可以比较真实和准确地反映企业本金化的价格，而且与投资决策紧密结合，因此，应用此法评估的资产价格易被买卖双方所接受。采用收益法进行资产评估的主要缺点是预期收益预测的难度较大，不仅受主观判断的影响，而且还受到未来收益不可预见因素的直接影响。

Questions and Problems

Choose the best answer to the following questions.

1. The value type for valuation is directly determined by (   ).

    A. valuation purpose.

    B. valuation approaches.

    C. valuation procedures.

    D. valuation basis.

2. What is the valuation subject? (   )

    A. Valuation institutions and personal.

    B. One side of trade.

    C. Valuation client.

    D. Auditor.

3. Which assumptions below is applied to liquidation value? (   )

    A. Open market assumption.

    B. Continue to use assumption.

    C. Liquidation assumption.

    D. Going concern assumption.

4. "The valuation institution and staff should be professional". This describes the (   ) characteristics of asset valuation.

    A. marketability.

    B. advisory.

    C. independence.

D. specialty.

5. "Both the valuation institution and certified asset appraisers should make an independent judgment of value of assets". This describes the (   ) characteristics of asset valuation.

A. marketability.

B. advisory.

C. independence.

D. specialty.

6. Which of the following assets can we not apply the cost approach to evaluate? (   )

A. Fixed assets.

B. Inventory.

C. Equipment.

D. Goodwill.

7. The deduction for cost method does not include (   ).

A. assets deduction.

B. functional deduction.

C. economic deduction.

D. physical deduction.

8. To apply the market approach, (   ) references should be taken into consideration.

A. equal to or more than 3.

B. more than 4.

C. 3.

D. less than 3.

9. Which of the following regarding income approach is not correct? (   )

A. Future income or cash flow could be forecasted and measured by currency.

B. The risk of future income for asset holders should be forecasted and measured.

C. The period of income should be forecast.

D. It is not necessary for discount rate to match future cash flow.

10. Which factor should be considered when estimating replacement cost? (   )

A. Purchase price.

B. Freight.

C. Necessary finance.

D. All the above.

Short answer questions.

1. What are the elements of asset valuation?
2. What are the characteristics of valuation?
3. What are the assumptions of valuation?
4. How many references should be selected when applying the market method, and why?

Numerical problems.

1. UO Company plans to purchase a fixed asset for operating. It is expected that the fixed asset will bring benefits of $150,000 per year in the first 6 years and the income will remain at a sustainable growth rate of 5% per year from the 7th year. The discount rate and capitalization rate is 10%.

Requirement: evaluate the value of the fixed asset.

2. BB Inc. company plans to purchase a set of second-hand manufacturing equipment. Its market price, related delivery cost and direct installation costs are $150,000, $40,000 and $10,000 respectively. In order to purchase the equipment, BB takes out a $150,000 1-year loan with CD bank with a 4% interest rate per year. The functional deduction and economic deduction related to the equipment are $8,000 and $7,000.

Requirement: estimate the value of the equipment.

3. KK Inc. company has a plant to be valued. Three comparable plants A, B, C can be found in the open market. The market prices of the three references are $1,000,000, $900,000 and $1,100,000 respectively. The convenient indexes of transportation of the valued plant and A, B, C are 8.7, 9, 8.5 and 9.4 respectively.

Requirement: estimate the value of plant of KK.

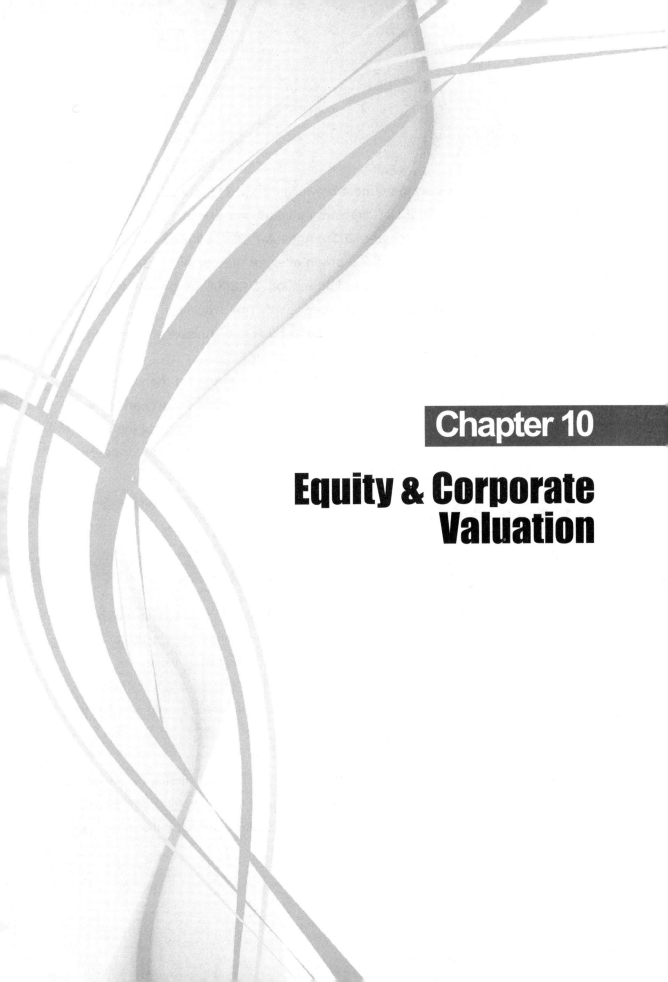

Chapter 10
Equity & Corporate Valuation

Introduction

Anheuser-Busch InBev, the largest brewer in the world, announced that it had intimated to SABMiller's board of directors its intentions to make a formal offer to acquire the company in September, 2015. Anheuser-Busch InBev mentioned that it intended to make a more than $100 billion offer for the company. SABMiller, the second largest brewer, confirmed this information. SABMiller's board of directors passed the acquisition proposal in September, 2016. The acquisition was completed successfully on October 10, 2016. The market value of Anheuser-Busch InBev increased to more than $200 billion after the acquisition.

It is known that the target of corporate finance is to maximize the shareholders' benefits or the enterprises' value. However, how can a company's equity and its value be evaluated? The discount cash flow model is mainly used to estimate the value of equity and firms. It involves two subsidiary models—dividend discount model and discount free cash flow model. Other methods are also to be introduced.

10.1 Equity Valuation

10.1.1 Dividends Discount Model

1. Overview of Dividend Discount Model

Stock is a vital element of the corporate valuation, especially for public corporations. The value of a stock is often used to indicate the value of the equity. The simplest model for valuing stock is the dividend discount model (DDM) — the value of a stock is the present value of expected dividends on it. Therefore the equity value could be the total value of shares(value of equity = value per share × number of shares). This chapter explores the general model as well as specific models for different assumptions to estimate shares' value.

2. The General Model

When investors buy stock, two types of cash flow — dividends during the period the stock is held and an expected price at the end of the holding period are obtained. Since this expected price itself is determined by future dividends, the value of a stock is the present value of dividends.

$$\text{Value per share} = \sum_{t=1}^{n} \frac{D}{(1+r)^t}$$

Value of equity = Value per share × Number of shares

Where: D = expected dividends per share;

r = cost of equity.

There are two basic concepts to the model. The first one is expected dividends, which is estimated by earnings and payout rations. The other is cost of equity—the required rate of return on a share determined by its riskiness, which is measured differently in different models. This chapter applies the capital asset pricing model(CAPM) to measure cost of equity.

3. Gordon Growth Model

Gordon growth model can be used to value a firm that is in a "steady state" with well-established dividend payout policies — dividends growing at a rate that can be sustained forever.

$$\text{Value per share} = \frac{D_1}{r-g} = \frac{D_0(1+g)}{r-g}$$

Value of equity = Value per share × Number of shares

Where: D_1 = expected dividends next period;

D_0 = expected dividends at present period;

r = consistent cost of equity;

g = expected stable growth rate in perpetuity and $r > g$.

While Gordon growth model is one of the most widely applied models in the field of stock valuation, it is limited to firms with a stable growth rate.

Two assumptions should be mentioned when estimating a stable growth rate. Firstly, since the growth rate of a firm's dividends is expected to last forever, the growth rate of the firm's other performance measurements (including earnings) should be in accord with that of dividends.

Secondly, in order to determine whether the dividends' growth rate of a company is suitable for the Gordon growth model, an estimate of the nominal economic growth rate, which is usually measured by nominal GDP (Gross Domestic Product) growth rate published by the authority, is needed. And it is generally equal or greater than the growth rate of the firm's dividends.

Example 10-1

Smith Inc. is a listed firm which produces mobiles and it has published 60,000,000 shares in the market. Smith appears to have a dividend policy of sustainable increases in rate of earnings, as well as dividends. The most recent dividend to pay is $1.5 per share and Smith forecasts that the dividends growth rate is 10% per year. The cost of its equity is 15% by using CAPM.

Requirement: calculate the value of Smith's equity by applying the Gordon growth model.

Solution:

$$\text{Value per share} = \frac{1.5 \times (1+10\%)}{15\% - 10\%} = \$33$$

Value of Smith's equity = 33 × 60,000,000 = $1,980,000,000

4. Two-stage Dividend Discount Model

Two growth periods are involved in the two-stage dividend discount model as shown in Figure 10-1 below. The initial phase is a period with an extraordinary growth rate, which will last n years. In this period, the growth rate is not stable and is usually higher than that during stage 2. The second period is called the sustainable stage. In this period, the growth rate is stable and is expected to remain in the long term or even forever. Additionally, the high growth rate in stage 1 transformed overnight to a lower stable rate at the end of the stage.

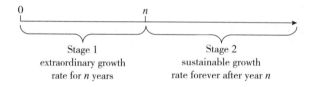

Figure 10-1 Two-stage dividend discount model

$$\text{Value per share} = \sum_{t=1}^{n} \frac{D_t}{(1+r_{hs})^t} + \frac{P_n}{(1+r_{hs})^n}$$

$$P_n = \frac{D_{n+1}}{r_{ns} - g_n}$$

Value of equity = Value per share × Number of shares

Where: D_t = expected dividends per share in year t;

r = cost of equity (hs: high growth period; ns: stable growth period);

P_n = present value at the end of year n;

g_n = growth rate forever after year n (stage 2).

The two-stage dividend discount model is suited for firms that are in high growth and expect to maintain that growth rate for a specific time period. The sources of the high growth are expected to disappear after this period.

Example 10-2

Smith Inc. plans to purchase THC company to extend its capacity in January, 2020. The information of THC is listed as below:

(1) THC is a listed enterprise and its number of shares outstanding is 10 million until 2020. THC is expected to deliver high growth in the next 5 years. After that, the sources of high growth are predicted to disappear and the company will maintain a stable growth rate forever more.

(2) Risk-free rate is 3.5%, and a mature market equity risk premium is 5%.

(3) It reported $160 million earnings for 2019 and paid out 25% of these earnings as dividends. On a per share basis, earnings were $16 and dividends were $4.

(4) The expected growth rate is 10% and the dividend payout ratio remains 25% in next 5 years.

(5) After year 5, the THC will be in a sustainable period with a growth rate of 5% and dividend payout ratio of 20%.

(6) The beta THC is 0.9 in the high growth period and it will move up to 1.2 in the stable period.

Requirement: estimate the value of THC's equity.

Solution:

$$\text{Cost of equity in high growth period} = 3.5\% + 0.9 \times 5\% = 8\%$$
$$\text{Cost of equity in stable growth period} = 3.5\% + 1.2 \times 5\% = 9.5\%$$

The value of high growth period is showed in Table 10-1 below.

Table 10-1 Present value in high growth period (Decimal to 2 places)

Year	2019	2020	2021	2022	2023	2024
Earnings per share	$16	$17.6	$19.36	$21.30	$23.43	$25.77
Payout ratio	25%	25%	25%	25%	25%	25%
Dividends per share	$4	$4.4	$4.84	$5.32	$5.85	$6.44
Cost of equity	8%	8%	8%	8%	8%	8%
Present value	—		$4.07	$4.14	$4.22	$4.29	$4.38

PV of dividends in high growth period = 4.07 + 4.14 + 4.22 + 4.29 + 4.38 = $21.1

$$\text{Value per share at the end of year 5} = \frac{25.77 \times (1+5\%) \times 20\%}{9.5\% - 5\%} = \$120.26$$

Value per share = PV of dividends in high growth period + Value per share at the end of year 5

$$= 21.1 + \frac{120.26}{(1+8\%)^5}$$
$$= \$102.95$$

Value of THC's equity = 102.95 × 10,000,000 = $1,029,500,000

10.1.2 Free Cash Flow to Equity Discount Model

In the dividend discount model, we value the equity by estimating the present value of expected dividends. The free cash flow to equity discount model tends to focus on the cash flow aspect. The value of equity is the present value of free cash flows to equity discounted by the cost of common equity.

1. What is the Free Cash Flow to Equity

Free cash flow to equity (FCFE) is the cash flow available to the company's common shareholders after all operating cash out flows, necessary investments paid, interest and principle paid to debt holders and dividends are payed for preferred stocks. FCFE is cash flow from operation minus capital expenditures, including long-term investment, increase in working capital, and the change of cash flow to debt holders and preferred shareholders.

2. Estimate Free Cash Flow to Equity

To estimate FCFE, several elements should be considered. Computing FCFE begins with accounting the net income. Non-cash charges, such as depreciation and amortization, should also be adjusted to add back as they are accrued but not cash expenses. Any capital expenditures including long-term investment and increase in net working capital should be deducted. Common stockholders also have to consider the effect of changes in debts cash flows. To repay the principal, cash will flow out the company. However, the repayment is always followed by issuing of new debt, which is a cash inflow. Finally, as the FCFE is focus on the cash flow of common equity investors, if the corporate issues the preferred stocks, the cash flow related to preferred stocks should be considered.

FCFE = Net income available to common shareholders (NI)
  + Net non-cash charges (NCC)
  − Long-term capital expenditures
  − Increase in net working capital
  + (New debt issued − Debt repayments)
  + (New preferred stock issued − Dividends of preference shares)

3. Implication of Discount Free Cash Flow to Equity Model

To estimate the value of a firm's equity, we can calculate the present value of the free cash flow of equity (FCFE).

$$Value\ of\ equity = \sum_{t=1}^{n} \frac{FCFE_t}{(1+r)^t}$$

Where: r = cost of equity reflecting the required return of common shareholders.

Equity & Corporate Valuation — Chapter 10

Example 10-3

Smith Inc. is a listed firm; the financial manager forecasts that the net income of Smith will be $50 million, $52 million, $51 million and $49 million from 2017 to 2020. The depreciation expense and working capital are 4% and 6% of its net income respectively. The working capital in 2016 is 1.5 million. Smith plans to invest in a $34 million long-term project in 2018. Additionally, Smith will repay the $12 million principle of debt in December 2019. And in order to the make repayment, Smith tends to issue a $10 million debt in December 2018. The cost of Smith's equity is 10%.

Requirement: estimate the equity value of Smith.

Solutions:

Forecast free cash flow of equity is showed in Table 10-2:

Table 10-2 Forecast free cash flow of equity (in millions)

Items	2017	2018	2019	2020
Net Income	$50	$52	$51	$49
Depreciation	$2	$2.08	$2.04	$1.96
Capital expenditure		$34		
Net working capital	$3	$3.12	$3.06	$2.94
Increase in net working capital	$1.5	$0.12	−$0.06	−$0.12
Cash flow to debts		$10	−$12	
Free cash flows of equity	$50.5	$29.96	$41.1	$51.08

$PV_{2017} = 50.5 \div (1+10\%) = \$45.91 \text{ million}$

$PV_{2018} = 29.96 \div (1+10\%)^2 = \$24.76 \text{ million}$

$PV_{2019} = 41.1 \div (1+10\%)^3 = \$30.88 \text{ million}$

$PV_{2020} = 51.08 \div (1+10\%)^4 = \$34.89 \text{ million}$

Value of Smith's equity = 45.91 + 24.76 + 30.88 + 34.89 = $136.44 million

10.2 Corporate Valuation

10.2.1 Free Cash Flow to the Firm Discount Model

1. Introduction to Free Cash Flow to the Firm Discount Model

The contexts we discussed above focus on the ordinary shareholders' benefits. The discounted free cash flow model goes one step further by determining the total value of a firm to all capital providers—both equity and debt holders. This section aims to provide a conceptual understanding of free cash flows and the valuation models based on them.

2. What is Free Cash Flow to the Firm?

Free cash flow to the firm (FCFF) is the cash flow available to capital suppliers of a firm after all operating expenses (including taxes) have been paid and necessary investment which includes working capital and long-term projects. The free cash flow to a firm is cash flow from operation minus capital expenditures. A firm's capital providers include bondholders, common stockholders and preferred stockholders.

3. Calculate Free Cash Flow From Net Income

To estimate how much cash can be afforded to the investors, accounting information should be appropriately applied. We should convert accounting measurements to a cash basis.

$$FCFF = \text{Net income available to common shareholders (NI)}$$
$$+ \text{Interest expense} \times (1 - \text{Tax rate})$$
$$+ \text{Net non-cash charges (NCC)}$$
$$- \text{Long-term capital expenditures}$$
$$- \text{Increase in net working capital}$$

Given every factor of FCFF, it begins at net income, which is reported in an income statement. Interest expenses after tax must be added back to net income because free cash flow of a firm represents the cash flow before pay to debt holders. Non-cash charges, such as depreciation and amortization, should also be adjusted to add back as they are accrued but are not cash expenses. Capital expenditures (long-term investment and increase in working capital) are subtracted from the net income as it with cash outflow.

> ***Example 10-4***
>
> THC, Inc. reported its 2019 financial statement in April, 2020. From the financial report, the net income for this year was $150,000 and it paid $10,000 interest expense to its debt. The net working capital in 2019 was $220,000 and it was $160,000 in 2018. In addition, the company invested in a new long-term capital of $100,000 in 2019. The new long-term capital is a depreciable property, which has a 10-year useful life with no salvage value. Other depreciation expenses for ASA are $20,000. The income tax rate is 25%.
>
> **Requirement:** calculate the free cash flow for THC in 2019.
>
> **Solution:**
>
> Depreciation expense of long-term investment per year = 100,000÷10 = $10,000
>
> Depreciation expense = 10,000 + 20,000 = $30,000
>
> Increase in net working capital = 220,000 − 160,000 = $60,000

$$\text{Free cash flow of THC} = 150{,}000 + 10{,}000 \times (1 - 25\%) + 30{,}000 - 100{,}000 - 60{,}000$$
$$= \$27{,}500$$

4. Finding FCFF from Earnings before Interest and Tax (EBIT)

FCFF always computes starting at net income. Another beginning is EBIT from the income statement.

To show the relationship between EBIT and FCFF, we firstly indicate the relationship between net income and EBIT.

The net income can be expressed as

$$\text{Net income} = (EBIT - \text{Interest expense}) \times (1 - \text{Tax rate})$$

Thus the FCFF could be referred as

$$FCFF = \text{Earnings before interest and tax} \times (1 - \text{Tax rate})$$
$$+ \text{Net noncash charges (NCC)}$$
$$- \text{Long-term capital expenditures}$$
$$- \text{Increase in net working capital}$$

5. Implication of Discount Free Cash Flow to Firm Model

To estimate the value of a firm's enterprise value, we can compute the present value of the free cash flow of firms (FCFF).

$$\text{Value of corporate} = \sum_{t=1}^{n} \frac{FCFF_t}{(1+r_{wacc})^t}$$

To apply this model, a key point that should be considered is the discount rate. In discount dividend model, we use cost of equity to calculate share value because we were discounting the cash flows owning to common shareholders. Here we are discounting the free cash flow to a firm that will be paid to both debt and equity holders. Thus, we should use the firm's weighted average cost of capital (WACC) as the discount rate to match the cash flows.

Example 10-5

Smith Inc. plans to sell its one subsidiary company FS in order to repay its debts on the basis of the following information:

(1) FS had sales of $518 million in 2016. And its EBIT was $344 million. The working capital was 5 million. In addition, the depreciation and amortization expenses were $30 million. The capital expenditure was $40 million in 2016. The income tax rate was 20%.

(2) Its sales are expected to grow at a 9% rate in 2017, but this growth rate will slow by 1% per year to a long-run growth rate for the apparel industry of 5% by the end of 2021.

(3) Based on FS past profitability and investment, it can be expected EBIT to be 15% of sales, capital expenditure to be 5% of sales, net working capital requirements to be 20% of any increase in sales, and depreciation and amortization expense to be 30% of any increase in sales from 2017 to 2021.

(4) FS maintains the asset-liability ratio of 50% and the cost of debt after tax is 7%, and the cost of equity is 13% during the period between 2017 and 2021.

(5) FS will step into a sustainable growth period with a growth rate at 4% on all items after 2021 and the situation will last forever. Other performance measurements will keep the same growth rate at 4% FS are expected to convert the asset-liability ratio to 40% with 8% cost of debt after tax and 10% cost of equity in 2022 and remain at this ratio during this period.

Requirement: what is the value of FS in early 2017?

Solutions:

Forecast free cash flow of FS (to 2 decimal places) is shown in Table 10-3.

Table 10-3 Forecast free cash flow of FS (in millions)

Items	2017	2018	2019	2020	2021	2022
Sales	$564.62	$609.79	$652.47	$691.62	$726.20	$755.25
Increase in sales	$46.62	$45.17	$42.69	$39.15	$34.58	$29.05
EBIT	$84.69	$91.47	$97.87	$103.74	$108.93	$113.29
Income tax	$16.94	$18.29	$19.57	$20.75	$21.79	$22.66
Depreciation & amortization	$13.99	$13.55	$12.81	$11.74	$10.37	$10.79
Capital expenditure	$28.23	$30.49	$32.62	$34.58	$36.31	$37.76
Net working capital	$9.32	$9.03	$8.54	$7.83	$6.92	$7.19
Increase in net working capital	$4.32	−$0.29	−$0.50	−$0.71	−$0.91	$0.28
Free cash flow of FS	$49.19	$56.53	$58.98	$60.87	$62.12	$63.38

$$WACC_{2017-2021} = 7\% \times 50\% + 13\% \times 50\% = 10\%$$

Present value 2017 —2021:

$PV_{2017} = 49.19 \div (1+10\%) = \$44.72$ million

$PV_{2018} = 56.53 \div (1+10\%)^2 = \$46.72$ million

$PV_{2019} = 58.98 \div (1+10\%)^3 = \$44.31$ million

$PV_{2020} = 60.87 \div (1+10\%)^4 = \$41.57$ million

$PV_{2021} = 62.12 \div (1+10\%)^5 = \$38.57$ million

Because the expected free cash flow to a constant rate after 2021, we can use the Gordon growth model to compute a terminal enterprise value:

WACC of stable growth period = 40% × 8% + 60% × 10% = 9.2%

The value of stable growth period at the end of 2021 = $\dfrac{63.38}{9.2\%-4\%}$ = $1,218.85 million

The current enterprise value is the present value of free cash flow of FS:

$$\text{Value of FS} = 44.72 + 46.72 + 44.31 + 41.57 + 38.57 + \dfrac{1{,}218.85}{(1+10\%)^5}$$

$$= \$972.70 \text{ million}$$

10.2.2 Price-Earnings Ratio

Price-earnings ratio (P/E ratio) is the ratio for valuing a company that measures its current share price relative to its earnings per share.

The P/E ratio can be calculated as:

$$P/E = \dfrac{Market\ price\ per\ share}{Earning\ per\ share}$$

Therefore, the current share price can be expressed as:

Market price per share = P/E × Earning per share

To apply P/E ratio, earning per share (EPS) estimating should be considered. Firstly, some particular effects such as unusual earnings should be eliminated. Secondly, as EPS is computed by accounting net income, accounting fraud may affect EPS. Additionally, if the company is affected by the business cycle, it should pay attention to the effects of different cycles (such as growth and recession) on EPS. Finally, if activities of authority of a company have an effect on the number of ordinary shares outside, the diluted earnings per share should be estimate.

In this chapter, we discussed the methods of equity and enterprise valuation. The analyst should apply the appropriate approach to estimate equity and a firm value based on the different facts associated with the specific company.

Core Words

dividends discount model (DDM)	股利折现模型
dividend payout ratio	股利支付率
two-stage dividend discount model	两阶段折现模型
free cash flow to equity (FCFE)	股权自由现金流量

debt holder	债权人
capital expenditure	资本性支出
non-cash charge	非现金支出
net working capital	净营运资本
free cash flow to firm (FCFF)	公司自由现金流量
earnings before interest and tax (EBIT)	息税前利润
weighted average cost of capital	加权平均资本成本
price-earnings ratio	市盈率
earnings per share (EPS)	每股收益
accounting fraud	会计舞弊
business cycle	商业周期

Key Concepts

1. Dividend discount model is one of the most popular methods to compute stock value by discounting future dividends to present value at the discount rate which is the cost of capital.

2. Gordon growth model is an approach to calculate the value of stocks with the dividend policy retaining a stable growth rate. where the growth rate is always less than the cost of equity.

3. Two-stage dividend discount model focuses on two periods. The dividends grow at extraordinary rate for several years during first period and then when the growth rate tends to be stable, it lasts forever. When estimating the value of share, dividends in both stages should be considered to discount to present value.

4. Free cash flow to equity discount model evaluates equity, from the view of cash flow. The cash flow to equity is the cash flow to common shareholders and it can be arrived at by adjusting accounting net income. The non-cash charges, capital expenditures and cash flow of debt holders and preference shareholders should be taken into account when making adjustment. To obtain the value of equity, the free cash flow should be discounted by the cost of common stocks.

5. For corporate valuation, free cash flow to the firm model is widely applied in this field. The company's value is the present value of its future free cash flow. The free cash flow is the cash flow to the capital suppliers, both debt holders and shareholders. To estimate the cash

flow, account net profit or earning before interest and tax should be adjusted. The discount rate for this model is the weighted average cost of capital to match the cash flow.

6. The price-earnings ratio (P/E ratio) is another method to evaluate a company. The market price of shares is equal to its P/E ratio multiplied by the earning per share.

Extended Reading

股利折现模型的局限性

股利折现模型是最常见的对权益进行评估的计算方法，但它在实际应用中存在着一些局限性。

第一，股利折现模型假设企业保持相对稳定的股利政策。但是，在企业的实际经营过程中，对于股利的发放存在着一定的不确定性。而且出于减少资本利得税的目的，企业会在一定程度上减少股利的发放，而选择将这部分资金留在企业进行再投资。有的企业甚至连续几年都不发放股利，在这种情况下，股利折现模型是不适用的。

第二，股利折现模型需要一个有效市场。所谓有效市场，是指市场价格包括了所有的信息，投资者可以获得全部的信息从而进行投资。而在实际中，这几乎是不可能实现的。投资者所得到的信息是片面的，市场中各主体之间的信息是不对称的，这在一定程度上会使股利折现模型应用的基础动摇。

市盈率的优缺点

市盈率在估价中得到了广泛应用，同时，对于P/E乘数也存在一定的争议。

应用市盈率具有如下优点。

第一，计算市盈率的数据容易取得，并且计算简单。

第二，市盈率把价格和收益联系起来，直观地反映投入和产出的关系。

第三，市盈率涵盖了风险补偿率、增长率、股利支付率的影响，具有很高的综合性。

应用市盈率的不足主要体现在以下几个方面。

第一，如果收益是负值，市盈率就失去了意义。这决定了市盈率的应用具有一定的局限性。

第二，会计政策的选择可能在一定程度上导致EPS的扭曲，进而导致不同公司间的P/E乘数缺乏可比性。

第三，市盈率除了受企业本身基本面的影响以外，还受到整体经济景气程度的影响。在经济繁荣时市盈率上升，经济衰退时市盈率下降，进而对投资的判断产生影响。

第四，在股票市场上，一个公司股票的市盈率可能会被非正常地提高或压低，因此无法反映公司资产的收益情况，从而很难正确地评估股票的价值。

Questions and Problems

Choose the best answer to the following questions.

1. Dividend models suggest that the value of a stock is determined by the (　　) holding it.

   A. present cash flows.

   B. past cash flows.

   C. future cash flows.

   D. past and present cash flows.

2. Constant growth dividend model requires that (　　).

   A. the return rate r is greater than the growth rate g of the dividend

   B. the return rate g is greater than the growth rate r of the dividend

   C. the return rate r is less than the growth rate g of the dividend

   D. the return rate r is equal to the growth rate g of the dividend

3. In Gordon growth model, the stable growth rate should be (　　) economic growth.

   A. not more than.

   B. not related to.

   C. equal to.

   D. less than.

4. To calculate the free cash flow to equity, which of the following conditions should be involved? (　　)

   A. Noncash charges.

   B. Debt.

   C. Accounting net income.

   D. All the above.

5. The last dividend (Div_0) is $2.80, the growth rate ($g$) is 8%, and the required rate of return (r) is 14%. What is the stock price according to the constant growth dividend model? (   )

A. $49.80

B. $46.67

C. $50.00

D. $50.40

6. Free cash flow to the firm is (   ).

A. cash flow to common shareholders

B. cash flow to all shareholders

C. cash flow to debt holders

D. cash flow to both debt holders and shareholders

7. The discount rate when computing the present value of the free cash flow to a firm, should be (   ).

A. cost of common shares

B. cost of equity

C. cost of debt

D. weighted average cost of capital

8. The value of shares will (   ) if the market interest rate increases.

A. increase

B. decrease

C. not change

D. none of the above

9. Which of the factors below is not related to the P/E ratio? (   )

A. Market price per shares

B. Net accounting income

C. Number of share outside

D. Liabilities

10. Which of the following statements is false? (   )

A. The free cash flow to a firm can be calculated by EBIT.

B. For two-stage model, the second period is always with a sustainable dividend growth rate which will last forever.

C. The cash flow should include the discount rate when estimating stock values.

D. When computing the stock value by Gordon growth model, the expected dividends at the present period should be discounted directly.

Numerical problems.

1. AA Inc., which is a listed firm appears to have a dividend policy of a sustainable increase rate of dividends, as well as earnings, The next period dividend to pay is $2 per share and it is expected that the dividends growth rate is 10% per year and the growth rate will continue forever. AA has 10 million shares. The cost of its equity is 13% by using CAPM.

Requirement: calculate the value of AA.

2. PP is a listed firm and it pays $3 per share to shareholders. PP has 20 million shares. It assumes that PP is expected to deliver a high growth rate at 10% in the next 4 years. After that, the sources of high growth are forecast to disappear and the company will maintain a stable growth rate at 8% forever. The cost of equity is 13% in the high growth period and 12% in the sustainable period.

Requirement: estimate the value of PP.

3. DQ Inc. had sales of $200 million in 2015. It is expecting its sales to grow at a 9% rate in 2016 and this will last for 5 years. Based on its past financial information, it expects EBIT to be 25% of sales, increases in net working capital to be 3% of EBIT, capital expenditure to be 4% of sales and depreciation to be 20% of capital expenditure. The average weighted cost of capital is 11% during the 5 years.

After 5 years, the growth rate converts to 5% on all elements and will last forever. The firm's cost of capital shifts to 12%.

Requirement: estimate the value of DQ.

4. TF Inc. plans to sell its one subsidiary company P&L in order to repay its debts on the basis of the following information:

(1) P&L had sales of $200 million in 2016. And its EBIT was $30 million. Interest expense is $12 million. The working capital was 5 million. In addition, the depreciation and amortization expense was $7 million. The capital expenditure was $16 million in 2016. The income tax rate was 25%.

(2) Its sales are expected to grow at a 10% rate in 2017, but that this growth rate will slow by 1% per year to a long-run growth rate for the apparel industry of 7% by the end of 2020.

(3) Based on P&L past profitability and investment, it expects EBIT to be 35% of sales, interest expense to be 7% of sales, capital expenditure to be 5% of sales, net working capital requirements to be 10% of any increase in sales, and depreciation and amortization expense to

be 9% of any increase in sales from 2017 to 2020.

(4) P&L forecasts that it will repay a $34 million loan in 2019 and due to the repayment, P&L takes out a $30 million new loan in the same year.

(5) The cost of equity is 12% during the period between 2017 and 2020.

(6) P&L will step into a sustainable growth period with a growth rate at 6% on all items after 2020 and the situation will last forever. P&L is expected to have 10% cost of equity in 2021 and remain at this ratio during this period.

Requirement: What is the value of P&L equity in early 2017?

Appendix I Future Value of $1 at Compound Interest

Periods	Interest rate									
	1%	2%	3%	4%	5%	6%	7%	8%	9%	10%
1	1.0100	1.0200	1.0300	1.0400	1.0500	1.0600	1.0700	1.0800	1.0900	1.1000
2	1.0201	1.0404	1.0609	1.0816	1.1025	1.1236	1.1449	1.1664	1.1881	1.2100
3	1.0303	1.0612	1.0927	1.1249	1.1576	1.1910	1.2250	1.2597	1.2950	1.3310
4	1.0406	1.0824	1.1255	1.1699	1.2155	1.2625	1.3108	1.3605	1.4116	1.4641
5	1.0510	1.1041	1.1593	1.2167	1.2763	1.3382	1.4026	1.4693	1.5386	1.6105
6	1.0615	1.1262	1.1941	1.2653	1.3401	1.4185	1.5007	1.5869	1.6771	1.7716
7	1.0721	1.1487	1.2299	1.3159	1.4071	1.5036	1.6058	1.7138	1.8280	1.9487
8	1.0829	1.1717	1.2668	1.3686	1.4775	1.5938	1.7182	1.8509	1.9926	2.1436
9	1.0937	1.1951	1.3048	1.4233	1.5513	1.6895	1.8385	1.9990	2.1719	2.3579
10	1.1046	1.2190	1.3439	1.4802	1.6289	1.7908	1.9672	2.1589	2.3674	2.5937
11	1.1157	1.2434	1.3842	1.5395	1.7103	1.8983	2.1049	2.3316	2.5804	2.8531
12	1.1268	1.2682	1.4258	1.6010	1.7959	2.0122	2.2522	2.5182	2.8127	3.1384
13	1.1381	1.2936	1.4685	1.6651	1.8856	2.1329	2.4098	2.7196	3.0658	3.4523
14	1.1495	1.3195	1.5126	1.7317	1.9799	2.2609	2.5785	2.9372	3.3417	3.7975
15	1.1610	1.3459	1.5580	1.8009	2.0789	2.3966	2.7590	3.1722	3.6425	4.1772
16	1.1726	1.3728	1.6047	1.8730	2.1829	2.5404	2.9522	3.4259	3.9703	4.5950
17	1.1843	1.4002	1.6528	1.9479	2.2920	2.6928	3.1588	3.7000	4.3276	5.0545
18	1.1961	1.4282	1.7024	2.0258	2.4066	2.8543	3.3799	3.9960	4.7171	5.5599
19	1.2081	1.4568	1.7535	2.1068	2.5270	3.0256	3.6165	4.3157	5.1417	6.1159
20	1.2202	1.4859	1.8061	2.1911	2.6533	3.2071	3.8697	4.6610	5.6044	6.7275
25	1.2824	1.6406	2.0938	2.6658	3.3864	4.2919	5.4274	6.8485	8.6231	10.8347
30	1.3478	1.8114	2.4273	3.2434	4.3219	5.7435	7.6123	10.0627	13.2677	17.4494
35	1.4166	1.9999	2.8139	3.9461	5.5160	7.6861	10.6766	14.7853	20.4140	28.1024
40	1.4889	2.2080	3.2620	4.8010	7.0400	10.2857	14.9745	21.7245	31.4094	45.2593

Future Value of $1 at Compound Interest Appendix I

(续表)

Periods	Interest rate									
	11%	12%	13%	14%	15%	16%	17%	18%	19%	20%
1	1.1100	1.1200	1.1300	1.1400	1.1500	1.1600	1.1700	1.1800	1.1900	1.2000
2	1.2321	1.2544	1.2769	1.2996	1.3225	1.3456	1.3689	1.3924	1.4161	1.4400
3	1.3676	1.4049	1.4429	1.4815	1.5209	1.5609	1.6016	1.6430	1.6852	1.7280
4	1.5181	1.5735	1.6305	1.6890	1.7490	1.8106	1.8739	1.9388	2.0053	2.0736
5	1.6851	1.7623	1.8424	1.9254	2.0114	2.1003	2.1924	2.2878	2.3864	2.4883
6	1.8704	1.9738	2.0820	2.1950	2.3131	2.4364	2.5652	2.6996	2.8398	2.9860
7	2.0762	2.2107	2.3526	2.5023	2.6600	2.8262	3.0012	3.1855	3.3793	3.5832
8	2.3045	2.4760	2.6584	2.8526	3.0590	3.2784	3.5115	3.7589	4.0214	4.2998
9	2.5580	2.7731	3.0040	3.2519	3.5179	3.8030	4.1084	4.4355	4.7854	5.1598
10	2.8394	3.1058	3.3946	3.7072	4.0456	4.4114	4.8068	5.2338	5.6947	6.1917
11	3.1518	3.4785	3.8359	4.2262	4.6524	5.1173	5.6240	6.1759	6.7767	7.4301
12	3.4985	3.8960	4.3345	4.8179	5.3503	5.9360	6.5801	7.2876	8.0642	8.9161
13	3.8833	4.3635	4.8980	5.4924	6.1528	6.8858	7.6987	8.5994	9.5964	10.6993
14	4.3104	4.8871	5.5348	6.2613	7.0757	7.9875	9.0075	10.1472	11.4198	12.8392
15	4.7846	5.4736	6.2543	7.1379	8.1371	9.2655	10.5387	11.9737	13.5895	15.4070
16	5.3109	6.1304	7.0673	8.1372	9.3576	10.7480	12.3303	14.1290	16.1715	18.4884
17	5.8951	6.8660	7.9861	9.2765	10.7613	12.4677	14.4265	16.6722	19.2441	22.1861
18	6.5436	7.6900	9.0243	10.5752	12.3755	14.4625	16.8790	19.6733	22.9005	26.6233
19	7.2633	8.6128	10.1974	12.0557	14.2318	16.7765	19.7484	23.2144	27.2516	31.9480
20	8.0623	9.6463	11.5231	13.7435	16.3665	19.4608	23.1056	27.3930	32.4294	38.3376
25	13.5855	17.0001	21.2305	26.4619	32.9190	40.8742	50.6578	62.6686	77.3881	95.3962
30	22.8923	29.9599	39.1159	50.9502	66.2118	85.8499	111.0647	143.3706	184.6753	237.3763
35	38.5749	52.7996	72.0685	98.1002	133.1755	180.3141	243.5035	327.9973	440.7006	590.6682
40	65.0009	93.0510	132.7816	188.8835	267.8635	378.7212	533.8687	750.3783	1051.6675	1469.7716

Appendix II   Present Value of $1 at Compound Interest

Periods	Interest rate									
	1%	2%	3%	4%	5%	6%	7%	8%	9%	10%
1	0.9901	0.9804	0.9709	0.9615	0.9524	0.9434	0.9346	0.9259	0.9174	0.9091
2	0.9803	0.9612	0.9426	0.9246	0.9070	0.8900	0.8734	0.8573	0.8417	0.8264
3	0.9706	0.9423	0.9151	0.8890	0.8638	0.8396	0.8163	0.7938	0.7722	0.7513
4	0.9610	0.9238	0.8885	0.8548	0.8227	0.7921	0.7629	0.7350	0.7084	0.6830
5	0.9515	0.9057	0.8626	0.8219	0.7835	0.7473	0.7130	0.6806	0.6499	0.6209
6	0.9420	0.8880	0.8375	0.7903	0.7462	0.7050	0.6663	0.6302	0.5963	0.5645
7	0.9327	0.8706	0.8131	0.7599	0.7107	0.6651	0.6227	0.5835	0.5470	0.5132
8	0.9235	0.8535	0.7894	0.7307	0.6768	0.6274	0.5820	0.5403	0.5019	0.4665
9	0.9143	0.8368	0.7664	0.7026	0.6446	0.5919	0.5439	0.5002	0.4604	0.4241
10	0.9053	0.8203	0.7441	0.6756	0.6139	0.5584	0.5083	0.4632	0.4224	0.3855
11	0.8963	0.8043	0.7224	0.6496	0.5847	0.5268	0.4751	0.4289	0.3875	0.3505
12	0.8874	0.7885	0.7014	0.6246	0.5568	0.4970	0.4440	0.3971	0.3555	0.3186
13	0.8787	0.7730	0.6810	0.6006	0.5303	0.4688	0.4150	0.3677	0.3262	0.2897
14	0.8700	0.7579	0.6611	0.5775	0.5051	0.4423	0.3878	0.3405	0.2992	0.2633
15	0.8613	0.7430	0.6419	0.5553	0.4810	0.4173	0.3624	0.3152	0.2745	0.2394
16	0.8528	0.7284	0.6232	0.5339	0.4581	0.3936	0.3387	0.2919	0.2519	0.2176
17	0.8444	0.7142	0.6050	0.5134	0.4363	0.3714	0.3166	0.2703	0.2311	0.1978
18	0.8360	0.7002	0.5874	0.4936	0.4155	0.3503	0.2959	0.2502	0.2120	0.1799
19	0.8277	0.6864	0.5703	0.4746	0.3957	0.3305	0.2765	0.2317	0.1945	0.1635
20	0.8195	0.6730	0.5537	0.4564	0.3769	0.3118	0.2584	0.2145	0.1784	0.1486
25	0.7798	0.6095	0.4776	0.3751	0.2953	0.2330	0.1842	0.1460	0.1160	0.0923
30	0.7419	0.5521	0.4120	0.3083	0.2314	0.1741	0.1314	0.0994	0.0754	0.0573
35	0.7059	0.5000	0.3554	0.2534	0.1813	0.1301	0.0937	0.0676	0.0490	0.0356
40	0.6717	0.4529	0.3066	0.2083	0.1420	0.0972	0.0668	0.0460	0.0318	0.0221

Present Value of $1 at Compound Interest

(续表)

Periods	Interest rate									
	11%	12%	13%	14%	15%	16%	17%	18%	19%	20%
1	0.9009	0.8929	0.8850	0.8772	0.8696	0.8621	0.8547	0.8475	0.8403	0.8333
2	0.8116	0.7972	0.7831	0.7695	0.7561	0.7432	0.7305	0.7182	0.7062	0.6944
3	0.7312	0.7118	0.6931	0.6750	0.6575	0.6407	0.6244	0.6086	0.5934	0.5787
4	0.6587	0.6355	0.6133	0.5921	0.5718	0.5523	0.5337	0.5158	0.4987	0.4823
5	0.5935	0.5674	0.5428	0.5194	0.4972	0.4761	0.4561	0.4371	0.4190	0.4019
6	0.5346	0.5066	0.4803	0.4556	0.4323	0.4104	0.3898	0.3704	0.3521	0.3349
7	0.4817	0.4523	0.4251	0.3996	0.3759	0.3538	0.3332	0.3139	0.2959	0.2791
8	0.4339	0.4039	0.3762	0.3506	0.3269	0.3050	0.2848	0.2660	0.2487	0.2326
9	0.3909	0.3606	0.3329	0.3075	0.2843	0.2630	0.2434	0.2255	0.2090	0.1938
10	0.3522	0.3220	0.2946	0.2697	0.2472	0.2267	0.2080	0.1911	0.1756	0.1615
11	0.3173	0.2875	0.2607	0.2366	0.2149	0.1954	0.1778	0.1619	0.1476	0.1346
12	0.2858	0.2567	0.2307	0.2076	0.1869	0.1685	0.1520	0.1372	0.1240	0.1122
13	0.2575	0.2292	0.2042	0.1821	0.1625	0.1452	0.1299	0.1163	0.1042	0.0935
14	0.2320	0.2046	0.1807	0.1597	0.1413	0.1252	0.1110	0.0985	0.0876	0.0779
15	0.2090	0.1827	0.1599	0.1401	0.1229	0.1079	0.0949	0.0835	0.0736	0.0649
16	0.1883	0.1631	0.1415	0.1229	0.1069	0.0930	0.0811	0.0708	0.0618	0.0541
17	0.1696	0.1456	0.1252	0.1078	0.0929	0.0802	0.0693	0.0600	0.0520	0.0451
18	0.1528	0.1300	0.1108	0.0946	0.0808	0.0691	0.0592	0.0508	0.0437	0.0376
19	0.1377	0.1161	0.0981	0.0829	0.0703	0.0596	0.0506	0.0431	0.0367	0.0313
20	0.1240	0.1037	0.0868	0.0728	0.0611	0.0514	0.0433	0.0365	0.0308	0.0261
25	0.0736	0.0588	0.0471	0.0378	0.0304	0.0245	0.0197	0.0160	0.0129	0.0105
30	0.0437	0.0334	0.0256	0.0196	0.0151	0.0116	0.0090	0.0070	0.0054	0.0042
35	0.0259	0.0189	0.0139	0.0102	0.0075	0.0055	0.0041	0.0030	0.0023	0.0017
40	0.0154	0.0107	0.0075	0.0053	0.0037	0.0026	0.0019	0.0013	0.0010	0.0007

Appendix III Present Value of an Annuity of $1 at Compound Interest

Periods	Interest rate									
	1%	2%	3%	4%	5%	6%	7%	8%	9%	10%
1	0.9901	0.9804	0.9709	0.9615	0.9524	0.9434	0.9346	0.9259	0.9174	0.9091
2	1.9704	1.9416	1.9135	1.8861	1.8594	1.8334	1.8080	1.7833	1.7591	1.7355
3	2.9410	2.8839	2.8286	2.7751	2.7232	2.6730	2.6243	2.5771	2.5313	2.4869
4	3.9020	3.8077	3.7171	3.6299	3.5460	3.4651	3.3872	3.3121	3.2397	3.1699
5	4.8534	4.7135	4.5797	4.4518	4.3295	4.2124	4.1002	3.9927	3.8897	3.7908
6	5.7955	5.6014	5.4172	5.2421	5.0757	4.9173	4.7665	4.6229	4.4859	4.3553
7	6.7282	6.4720	6.2303	6.0021	5.7864	5.5824	5.3893	5.2064	5.0330	4.8684
8	7.6517	7.3255	7.0197	6.7327	6.4632	6.2098	5.9713	5.7466	5.5348	5.3349
9	8.5660	8.1622	7.7861	7.4353	7.1078	6.8017	6.5152	6.2469	5.9952	5.7590
10	9.4713	8.9826	8.5302	8.1109	7.7217	7.3601	7.0236	6.7101	6.4177	6.1446
11	10.3676	9.7868	9.2526	8.7605	8.3064	7.8869	7.4987	7.1390	6.8052	6.4951
12	11.2551	10.5753	9.9540	9.3851	8.8633	8.3838	7.9427	7.5361	7.1607	6.8137
13	12.1337	11.3484	10.6350	9.9856	9.3936	8.8527	8.3577	7.9038	7.4869	7.1034
14	13.0037	12.1062	11.2961	10.5631	9.8986	9.2950	8.7455	8.2442	7.7862	7.3667
15	13.8651	12.8493	11.9379	11.1184	10.3797	9.7122	9.1079	8.5595	8.0607	7.6061
16	14.7179	13.5777	12.5611	11.6523	10.8378	10.1059	9.4466	8.8514	8.3126	7.8237
17	15.5623	14.2919	13.1661	12.1657	11.2741	10.4773	9.7632	9.1216	8.5436	8.0216
18	16.3983	14.9920	13.7535	12.6593	11.6896	10.8276	10.0591	9.3719	8.7556	8.2014
19	17.2260	15.6785	14.3238	13.1339	12.0853	11.1581	10.3356	9.6036	8.9501	8.3649
20	18.0456	16.3514	14.8775	13.5903	12.4622	11.4699	10.5940	9.8181	9.1285	8.5136
25	22.0232	19.5235	17.4131	15.6221	14.0939	12.7834	11.6536	10.6748	9.8226	9.0770
30	25.8077	22.3965	19.6004	17.2920	15.3725	13.7648	12.4090	11.2578	10.2737	9.4269
35	29.4086	24.9986	21.4872	18.6646	16.3742	14.4982	12.9477	11.6546	10.5668	9.6442
40	32.8347	27.3555	23.1148	19.7928	17.1591	15.0463	13.3317	11.9246	10.7574	9.7791

Present Value of an Annuity of $1 at Compound Interest

(续表)

Periods	Interest rate									
	11%	12%	13%	14%	15%	16%	17%	18%	19%	20%
1	0.9009	0.8929	0.8850	0.8772	0.8696	0.8621	0.8547	0.8475	0.8403	0.8333
2	1.7125	1.6901	1.6681	1.6467	1.6257	1.6052	1.5852	1.5656	1.5465	1.5278
3	2.4437	2.4018	2.3612	2.3216	2.2832	2.2459	2.2096	2.1743	2.1399	2.1065
4	3.1024	3.0373	2.9745	2.9137	2.8550	2.7982	2.7432	2.6901	2.6386	2.5887
5	3.6959	3.6048	3.5172	3.4331	3.3522	3.2743	3.1993	3.1272	3.0576	2.9906
6	4.2305	4.1114	3.9975	3.8887	3.7845	3.6847	3.5892	3.4976	3.4098	3.3255
7	4.7122	4.5638	4.4226	4.2883	4.1604	4.0386	3.9224	3.8115	3.7057	3.6046
8	5.1461	4.9676	4.7988	4.6389	4.4873	4.3436	4.2072	4.0776	3.9544	3.8372
9	5.5370	5.3282	5.1317	4.9464	4.7716	4.6065	4.4506	4.3030	4.1633	4.0310
10	5.8892	5.6502	5.4262	5.2161	5.0188	4.8332	4.6586	4.4941	4.3389	4.1925
11	6.2065	5.9377	5.6869	5.4527	5.2337	5.0286	4.8364	4.6560	4.4865	4.3271
12	6.4924	6.1944	5.9176	5.6603	5.4206	5.1971	4.9884	4.7932	4.6105	4.4392
13	6.7499	6.4235	6.1218	5.8424	5.5831	5.3423	5.1183	4.9095	4.7147	4.5327
14	6.9819	6.6282	6.3025	6.0021	5.7245	5.4675	5.2293	5.0081	4.8023	4.6106
15	7.1909	6.8109	6.4624	6.1422	5.8474	5.5755	5.3242	5.0916	4.8759	4.6755
16	7.3792	6.9740	6.6039	6.2651	5.9542	5.6685	5.4053	5.1624	4.9377	4.7296
17	7.5488	7.1196	6.7291	6.3729	6.0472	5.7487	5.4746	5.2223	4.9897	4.7746
18	7.7016	7.2497	6.8399	6.4674	6.1280	5.8178	5.5339	5.2732	5.0333	4.8122
19	7.8393	7.3658	6.9380	6.5504	6.1982	5.8775	5.5845	5.3162	5.0700	4.8435
20	7.9633	7.4694	7.0248	6.6231	6.2593	5.9288	5.6278	5.3527	5.1009	4.8696
25	8.4217	7.8431	7.3300	6.8729	6.4641	6.0971	5.7662	5.4669	5.1951	4.9476
30	8.6938	8.0552	7.4957	7.0027	6.5660	6.1772	5.8294	5.5168	5.2347	4.9789
35	8.8552	8.1755	7.5856	7.0700	6.6166	6.2153	5.8582	5.5386	5.2512	4.9915
40	8.9511	8.2438	7.6344	7.1050	6.6418	6.2335	5.8713	5.5482	5.2582	4.9966

Appendix IV Future Value of an Annuity of $1 at Compound Interest

Periods	Interest rate									
	1%	2%	3%	4%	5%	6%	7%	8%	9%	10%
1	1.0000	1.0000	1.0000	1.0000	1.0000	1.0000	1.0000	1.0000	1.0000	1.0000
2	2.0100	2.0200	2.0300	2.0400	2.0500	2.0600	2.0700	2.0800	2.0900	2.1000
3	3.0301	3.0604	3.0909	3.1216	3.1525	3.1836	3.2149	3.2464	3.2781	3.3100
4	4.0604	4.1216	4.1836	4.2465	4.3101	4.3746	4.4399	4.5061	4.5731	4.6410
5	5.1010	5.2040	5.3091	5.4163	5.5256	5.6371	5.7507	5.8666	5.9847	6.1051
6	6.1520	6.3081	6.4684	6.6330	6.8019	6.9753	7.1533	7.3359	7.5233	7.7156
7	7.2135	7.4343	7.6625	7.8983	8.1420	8.3938	8.6540	8.9228	9.2004	9.4872
8	8.2857	8.5830	8.8923	9.2142	9.5491	9.8975	10.2598	10.6366	11.0285	11.4359
9	9.3685	9.7546	10.1591	10.5828	11.0266	11.4913	11.9780	12.4876	13.0210	13.5795
10	10.4622	10.9497	11.4639	12.0061	12.5779	13.1808	13.8164	14.4866	15.1929	15.9374
11	11.5668	12.1687	12.8078	13.4864	14.2068	14.9716	15.7836	16.6455	17.5603	18.5312
12	12.6825	13.4121	14.1920	15.0258	15.9171	16.8699	17.8885	18.9771	20.1407	21.3843
13	13.8093	14.6803	15.6178	16.6268	17.7130	18.8821	20.1406	21.4953	22.9534	24.5227
14	14.9474	15.9739	17.0863	18.2919	19.5986	21.0151	22.5505	24.2149	26.0192	27.9750
15	16.0969	17.2934	18.5989	20.0236	21.5786	23.2760	25.1290	27.1521	29.3609	31.7725
16	17.2579	18.6393	20.1569	21.8245	23.6575	25.6725	27.8881	30.3243	33.0034	35.9497
17	18.4304	20.0121	21.7616	23.6975	25.8404	28.2129	30.8402	33.7502	36.9737	40.5447
18	19.6147	21.4123	23.4144	25.6454	28.1324	30.9057	33.9990	37.4502	41.3013	45.5992
19	20.8109	22.8406	25.1169	27.6712	30.5390	33.7600	37.3790	41.4463	46.0185	51.1591
20	22.0190	24.2974	26.8704	29.7781	33.0660	36.7856	40.9955	45.7620	51.1601	57.2750
25	28.2432	32.0303	36.4593	41.6459	47.7271	54.8645	63.2490	73.1059	84.7009	98.3471
30	34.7849	40.5681	47.5754	56.0849	66.4388	79.0582	94.4608	113.2832	136.3075	164.4940
35	41.6603	49.9945	60.4621	73.6522	90.3203	111.4348	138.2369	172.3168	215.7108	271.0244
40	48.8864	60.4020	75.4013	95.0255	120.7998	154.7620	199.6351	259.0565	337.8824	442.5926

Future Value of an Annuity of $1 at Compound Interest

(续表)

Periods	Interest rate									
	11%	12%	13%	14%	15%	16%	17%	18%	19%	20%
1	1.0000	1.0000	1.0000	1.0000	1.0000	1.0000	1.0000	1.0000	1.0000	1.0000
2	2.1100	2.1200	2.1300	2.1400	2.1500	2.1600	2.1700	2.1800	2.1900	2.2000
3	3.3421	3.3744	3.4069	3.4396	3.4725	3.5056	3.5389	3.5724	3.6061	3.6400
4	4.7097	4.7793	4.8498	4.9211	4.9934	5.0665	5.1405	5.2154	5.2913	5.3680
5	6.2278	6.3528	6.4803	6.6101	6.7424	6.8771	7.0144	7.1542	7.2966	7.4416
6	7.9129	8.1152	8.3227	8.5355	8.7537	8.9775	9.2068	9.4420	9.6830	9.9299
7	9.7833	10.0890	10.4047	10.7305	11.0668	11.4139	11.7720	12.1415	12.5227	12.9159
8	11.8594	12.2997	12.7573	13.2328	13.7268	14.2401	14.7733	15.3270	15.9020	16.4991
9	14.1640	14.7757	15.4157	16.0853	16.7858	17.5185	18.2847	19.0859	19.9234	20.7989
10	16.7220	17.5487	18.4197	19.3373	20.3037	21.3215	22.3931	23.5213	24.7089	25.9587
11	19.5614	20.6546	21.8143	23.0445	24.3493	25.7329	27.1999	28.7551	30.4035	32.1504
12	22.7132	24.1331	25.6502	27.2707	29.0017	30.8502	32.8239	34.9311	37.1802	39.5805
13	26.2116	28.0291	29.9847	32.0887	34.3519	36.7862	39.4040	42.2187	45.2445	48.4966
14	30.0949	32.3926	34.8827	37.5811	40.5047	43.6720	47.1027	50.8180	54.8409	59.1959
15	34.4054	37.2797	40.4175	43.8424	47.5804	51.6595	56.1101	60.9653	66.2607	72.0351
16	39.1899	42.7533	46.6717	50.9804	55.7175	60.9250	66.6488	72.9390	79.8502	87.4421
17	44.5008	48.8837	53.7391	59.1176	65.0751	71.6730	78.9792	87.0680	96.0218	105.9306
18	50.3959	55.7497	61.7251	68.3941	75.8364	84.1407	93.4056	103.7403	115.2659	128.1167
19	56.9395	63.4397	70.7494	78.9692	88.2118	98.6032	110.2846	123.4135	138.1664	154.7400
20	64.2080	72.0524	80.9468	91.0249	102.4436	115.3797	130.0329	146.6280	165.4180	186.6880
25	114.4133	133.3339	155.6196	181.8708	212.7930	249.2140	292.1049	342.6035	402.0425	471.9811
30	199.0209	241.3327	293.1992	356.7868	434.7451	530.3117	647.4391	790.9480	966.7122	1181.8816
35	341.5896	431.6635	546.6808	693.5727	881.1702	1120.7130	1426.4910	1816.6516	2314.2137	2948.3411
40	581.8261	767.0914	1013.7042	1342.0251	1779.0903	2360.7572	3134.5218	4163.2130	5529.8290	7343.8578